WHEN CAN
I RETIRE?

Also by Andrew Allentuck

Consumer Choice: The Economics of Personal Living
(co-authored with Gordon Bivens)

The Cost of Age

Who Speaks for the Patient?

Bonds for Canadians:
How to Build Wealth and Lower Risk in Your Portfolio

WHEN CAN
I RETIRE?

Planning Your Financial Life After Work

Andrew
Allentuck

VIKING
CANADA

VIKING CANADA

Published by the Penguin Group

Penguin Group (Canada), 90 Eglinton Avenue East, Suite 700,
Toronto, Ontario, Canada M4P 2Y3 (a division of Pearson Canada Inc.)

Penguin Group (USA) Inc., 375 Hudson Street, New York, New York 10014, U.S.A.
Penguin Books Ltd, 80 Strand, London WC2R 0RL, England
Penguin Ireland, 25 St Stephen's Green, Dublin 2, Ireland (a division of Penguin Books Ltd)
Penguin Group (Australia), 250 Camberwell Road, Camberwell, Victoria 3124, Australia
(a division of Pearson Australia Group Pty Ltd)
Penguin Books India Pvt Ltd, 11 Community Centre, Panchsheel Park,
New Delhi – 110 017, India
Penguin Group (NZ), 67 Apollo Drive, Rosedale, North Shore 0632, Auckland, New Zealand
(a division of Pearson New Zealand Ltd)
Penguin Books (South Africa) (Pty) Ltd, 24 Sturdee Avenue, Rosebank,
Johannesburg 2196, South Africa

Penguin Books Ltd, Registered Offices: 80 Strand, London WC2R 0RL, England

First published 2009

1 2 3 4 5 6 7 8 9 10 (RRD)

Copyright © Andrew Allentuck, 2009

Manufactured in the U.S.A.

Library and Archives Canada Cataloguing in Publication data available
upon request to the publisher.

ISBN: 978-0-670-06793-0

Visit the Penguin Group (Canada) website at **www.penguin.ca**

Special and corporate bulk purchase rates available; please see
www.penguin.ca/corporatesales or call 1-800-810-3104, ext. 477 or 474

For Adam and Kate, Sarah and Dov

Contents

Preface:
A Journey Together

The question "When can I retire?" is the most frequent and surely one of the most complex that people ask as they move through life from starting work to ending it. The problem of planning not to work is, in fact, a web of issues that involves budgeting for many years, the problem and uncertainty of mortality, deciding how much money to leave to children or to others, investment returns, and, of course, the very personal problem of what one will do with years of leisure time. It is a one-way decision for most of us and among the most important that we will ever make.

Retirement planning and the question of timing retirement require an assessment of one's capital, the desire to quit conventional work, and sufficient resources to cope with years or decades of life without a time sheet or need to show up at an office. The earlier one retires, the harder it is to see ahead. In truth, predicting anything more than a few months in the future is tough. Predicting what the financial world will be like in 10 or 20 or 30 years is nearly impossible. But it has to be done and, as I try to show in *When Can I Retire?*, it is best done with a sharp pencil and conservative assumptions. After all, to reach the last years of life flat broke is tragic.

There is a lot of such tragedy. I have examined many cases of poverty in old age through the Financial Facelift series of personal financial planning stories that I have written for the Toronto *Globe and Mail* since 2000. I have heard from people who have drifted into poverty by failure to plan for the gift of a long life. That is regrettable, of course. Yet it is relatively rare for people to have nothing. After all, Canada's combination of Old Age Security enhanced by the Guaranteed Income Supplement ensures a modest level of income for almost every person age 65 or older.

People approaching old age understandably fear poverty. University students, with the hope of a career to come, find that poverty is bearable. But for the elderly, with little chance of generating large incomes late in life, poverty is harder to bear. Not surprisingly, it is dreaded.

The basis for fear is less logic than what Franklin Roosevelt identified as the cause of gloom for America's future in the Great Depression when he said, "We have nothing to fear but fear itself." That insight is worth a heap of psychology books, for when one can take decades to plan a life of work and a life after work, rationality should work.

It should, but the complexity of paying one's current bills, coping with investments and the legions of companies that sell insurance and mutual funds, paying for children's music lessons and hockey practice and then university fees, and shepherding children into lives of their own seems to obscure the basic task of salting away enough capital to provide an acceptable way of life for a few decades after the end of formal work.

Myopia—short-sightedness—is one reason it seems so hard to build up capital. Stock markets gyrate every day and week, month and year, but over time, they go up more than they go down. Ignore the wobbles and the outcome should be benevolent, even if it cannot be quantified years or even decades in advance of retirement. Bonds can produce dependable interest flow that, if compounded, can produce handsome fortunes over periods of many decades. If it is so easy, why should we need a book to get through the process?

The fundamentals are not the issue. Bureaucratic and legal complexity is. Tax law and rules for pension funds, international treaties for persons in one benefit plan living in another country, inflation and the variability of exchange rates that affect one's ability to live in Florida or France turn every retirement planner into a negotiator, trading certainty of bond income for the perhaps higher if riskier gains of investing in the stock market.

The earlier you retire, the more financial circumstance—wealth, responsibilities, and rates of return on assets—may change over time. If you cease work at age 80, your capital need last a shorter period than if you retire at age 50. Fortunately, stock markets tend to produce the best and least variable performance over long periods. It is the short run that is in doubt. Early retirement allows less time to save for retirement, but once retired, if one can preserve capital, it is likely to produce large gains in periods of two or more decades.

When Can I Retire? is intended to speak to every person contemplating retirement. The issues of retirement planning, though substantially financial, begin with the reasons for quitting work in a formal sense. Over the last few decades, compulsory retirement at a fixed age has withered in law and in advances in health that extended life expectancy. The idea, prevalent early in the 20th century, that one might quit work at 65 and have a few pleasant years of well-earned leisure before dying, has given way to the new reality that retirement at 55 or 60 or 65 will leave perhaps two or three decades of leisure or boredom before death.

The psychological component of retirement cannot be ignored. Indeed, the concept of oldness is changing. A new word, "tweeniors," describes those between 55 and 70, with the ages as flexible as those who use the term. It implies that 55 is too old to be middle-aged and 65 to 69 too young to be a senior. As time goes on and the proportion of persons over 65 to total population grows, you can expect further changes in the words that define oldness and pensionability. The young who plan for the future and care about the time when they no longer work or work much will eventually have to redefine when retirement begins. Clearly, that period is due to begin later in life.

The problem of financing retirement is complex when we think of a period as short even as 5 years. We can make intelligent forecasts of the range of interest rates for a few years. At 10 years, the fog gets thicker. At 30 years, financial planning becomes intelligent extrapolation and reliance on financial history. In the hands of modest and experienced advisors, it can be done to provide assurances of ranges of buying power and expectations of income. But predicting inflation rates three decades hence or the cost of housing or cars or, for that matter, a dozen eggs is more fortune-telling than economics.

I have written *When Can I Retire?* as a manual, a shelf reference if you like. It is free of fictitious stories of proxy retirees and advisors. The storytelling style of personal finance was made popular by such bestsellers as *The Wealthy Barber*. The success of these books in the market may be a recommendation for other authors to follow them. However, it is my belief that fiction has no part in financial books. To those who like such content, I offer my regrets, for I have chosen clarity over the diversion of allegory.

Retirement planning is really many fields combined into one concern. It is an area of active law reform and frequent legislative change. Amounts payable as government pensions change often. As well, principles governing benefits evolve frequently with exceptions to rules complicating the broad rules. I have tried to find a balance of readability and comprehensiveness. In many cases, I have had to leave subcases of rules and special exceptions to footnotes and references to relevant websites. Readers should check those references to get current information on situations that are of concern to them. It may also be wise to seek counsel from financial planners or other advisors in tax, law, insurance annuities, pensions, and investments. In every case where an important decision is to be made, it is vital to obtain current information from relevant sources on the web, in human resources departments in companies that provide pension income, and from tax professionals.

How to Use This Book

The problem of timing retirement consists in finding at what time—now or some point in the future—what you have available to spend will match what you need to spend. The problem of figuring out when this will happen therefore has two clear parts.

Readers may approach the problem from either end, but it is necessary to examine both spending and income. You may want to go from front to back, following the logic of the text. Alternatively, you may just skip the larger questions and go directly to balancing expense and income.

Chapter 1 is an introduction to the problems of planning retirement.

Chapter 2 examines the issues in retirement. This chapter sets the stage for planning with regard to life expectancy and considers when you should start the process in earnest.

Chapter 3 discusses the pros and cons of retiring.

Chapter 4 examines personal spending by stage of retirement and sets out a method for estimating costs by stage of life. The chapter covers housing costs and spending for food, transportation, travel, health care, charities, and gifts. The chapter then sets out a method for estimating expenses by stage of life from early old age—65 to 75—and later old age—75 to 85 and beyond.

Chapter 5 examines public pensions for retirement. We review public pensions such as Old Age Security, the Canada and Quebec Pension Plans, and the Guaranteed Income Supplement.

Chapter 6 analyzes employment-based pensions, defined benefit and defined contribution pensions, various individual pension schemes, Registered Retirement Savings Plans and Registered Retirement Income Funds, and annuities and Tax-Free Savings Accounts.

Chapter 7 shows how persons approaching retirement, saving for retirement, or already retired can increase their income through a variety of investment strategies.

Chapter 8 tries to anticipate what you will do with decades of free time.

Chapter 9 provides resources for coping with the phenomenon that uncertainty grows over time.

Chapter 10 will assist those who are considering retirement in the United States or in other countries. It offers a list of pluses and minuses for deciding whether to retire and when to do it.

Chapter 11 demonstrates that retirement as we know it may be withering in favour of extended years of conventional employment.

The glossary provides terms that may be useful for the reader.

WHEN CAN
I RETIRE?

Chapter 1

Retirement: The Destination and the Trouble of Getting There

Retirement, often seen as a reward for a life of work and the destiny of a career, is part myth and part reality. It can be decades of golf and friendship, seeing grandchildren grow up and go to university, travel abroad and other pleasures. That is the retirement of the relatively few people who have been fortunate enough to rise to the top of organizations that provide six- and even seven-figure annual pensions or who have had the luck and good fortune to prosper in the stock market. For the remainder of folks who have left the labour force, retirement is often a time of apprehension and fear of want.

The fear is well founded, for when a career or job is finished, most of us face the need to live on what we have built in capital, work pensions, and entitlements to public pensions. The situation can be downright frightening. And it ought to be. The odds of getting a high-paying job in your late sixties or seventies are slight.

We hear of new career starts, but they are little more than rare anecdotes. For most retirees, the period that follows work is one not of abundance, but of measured privation.

It was not supposed to be this way. The idea of retirement is really a newfangled thing, traceable back to late 19th century German roots when a few years of idleness were to be a reward for decades of backbreaking toil. Pension systems grew with the idea that the few who might survive to age 65 would be rewarded for their luck or prudence in healthy living.

With the extension of life far beyond 65 and with the likelihood of good health in many of those years, the problem is no longer survival on a pittance, but living reasonably well for what may be decades of life after leaving formal or at least previous work. Today, the issue in retirement planning is how to fund and manage years of dependence when public pensions such as Canada's Old Age Security and the various entitlement programs bundled up as social security seem inadequate. After all, most pension plans pay the average retiree relatively little. Building up a large nest egg through wise investment remains an opportunity and a challenge.

The fear that there will be no money left when we are elderly and dependent on others haunts many of us. A poll by Decima Research reported by the Canadian Press showed that a third of Canadian senior and almost-senior citizens fear that they will outlive their money. The July 15, 2007, survey showed that 44 percent of respondents said they were not worried about outliving their financial resources while 33 percent said they were worried. The remainder, presumably, did not care enough to have a firm opinion. The Decima Research poll was conducted on a select group of persons responding to questions online. That group is, of course, more likely to be educated and have higher incomes than others who do not have computer access or computing skills.

Mel Rempel, 58, quit working as a stationary engineer for the University of Manitoba and took what amounted to an early retirement in 2004. He says that "what keeps people working is fear of poverty." A deeply thoughtful man who reads philosophy and history as a pastime, he explains that financial planning is a choice that most of those considering retirement don't have. "They have to take what comes from public pensions. They do not have the luxury of working up investment plans. After all, when you have a low income, you really can't save very much."

QUESTION: Should you be afraid of poverty in old age?

ANSWER: The advantage of being insecure is that you can do something about it before it happens. Reading this book is a part of that process. Congratulations for taking a first step.

For most people, the idea of a retirement of the sort pictured in *Architectural Digest*—life on a yacht or in a mansion surrounded by a vineyard—is unattainable. That level of lavish living requires annual incomes well into six or seven figures. But Canadians, ironically, have a better chance of having a comfortable retirement than Americans. After all, bankruptcy by reason of medical or drug expense is an infrequent problem in Canada. In the United States, personal bankruptcies among persons over age 55 are rising, driven by health care costs and mortgage debt.[1] In Canada, publicly funded health care provides benefits that grow in value as people get older.

To Be Old Is Often to Be Poor

Government-funded medical care is of immense importance to older Canadians, especially those who have retired and find their incomes fixed. A Statistics Canada study, *The Assets and Debts of Canadians: An Overview of the Results of the Survey of Financial Security*, reported that, as the new millennium opened, the dominant financial characteristic of families headed by a senior citizen was low income. The median after-tax income of senior families was $32,000, $12,400 lower than for families headed by a non-senior citizen.[2]

Pre-tax income of $32,000 will pay for groceries and limited travel, modest presents for children and grandchildren, utility bills and minor home repairs, and clothing bought on a budget. For retirees who have paid for their homes and no longer have to fund their RRSPs or other pension plans, it's enough to get by. But it's only that.

In a study entitled "Planning for Retirement: Are Canadians Saving Enough?" prepared by the Department of Statistics and Actuarial Science at the University of Waterloo and released June 14, 2007, Robert L. Brown and colleagues demonstrate that two-thirds of Canadians now in their early to mid-forties will have difficulty as retirees paying for basics unless they increase their rate of savings or are prepared to keep working past age 65.[3]

The problem is that two-thirds of Canadian households anticipating retirement in 2030 are not saving enough money to meet their expected living expenses, the actuaries report. Old Age Security and the Canada/Quebec Pension Plan, work-related pensions, and even the monetization of homes by sale or remortgaging will not be enough to keep up with inflation, the report implies.

The University of Waterloo study concluded that a single person earning $40,000 per year needs to save between 14 and 20 percent of annual income to pay for basic expenses in retirement. A couple with a total income of $40,000 needs to save at least 30 percent of annual income. The goals are obviously difficult to attain. The report allows for some grace, however, for a sensible investment plan can boost cash savings over the years leading up to 2030.

For those who do not put together the resources to finance a secure retirement, the alternative is continuation of work. One can take a benign view of working later than 65. After all, a life of inactivity is likely to produce unhappiness, perhaps overindulgence in alcohol, and even early death.

Working after the traditional retirement age raises the question of what kind of work you can do and, even more, whether you have the ability to keep on working. A plan to work to age 70 or 75 can be altered by the reality of health issues.

Life Expectancy and Health Expectations

"Planning for retirement is more than about just money, it's also about health," says Guy Patton, executive director of the Fidelity Research Institute in Boston, a unit of Fidelity Investments, one of the largest mutual fund vendors and managers in the United States. "One can impact the other."[4]

Life expectancy is rising and, with it, the income gap that has to be filled with pensions or investment income. Moreover, even though life expectancy is growing, health expectancy is not keeping up. There remains a good chance that you will be infirm or too ill to work toward the end of life. Moreover, the practice of many financial planners of setting a date of life expectancy plus five years as the point at which a person's assets will be exhausted can leave the retiree flat broke just when he or she is unable to work.

The problem is that a plan for death may be redeemed by life. The ironic result that the survivor's good luck leaves him or her in poverty can be resolved by ensuring that withdrawals from savings in the form of investment accounts or registered retirement income funds or the sale of assets like houses always leaves a substantial amount of capital at work.

Not everyone can afford to leave capital intact or even growing at a rate that compensates for inflation. The alternative is to buy a life annuity with a part of your capital. Life annuities pay income for a designated length of time, usually for the life or the lives of both spouses, sometimes with a minimum payment guarantee so that a premature death will not cause a large financial loss. Based on bonds, life annuities are like mortgages running in reverse with no fixed terminal date. In theory, they pay interest and use up capital, but the insurance companies that sell them take the risk that you will live longer than average. As insurance against poverty, annuities have a vital role to play for retirees who fear they will outlast their money.

QUESTION: Is it possible to insure against illness and poverty?

ANSWER: No to illness but yes to the costs of both. Government health and drug plans cover most of the costs of illness, and supplemental health plans can cover nearly all the rest. The risk of poverty in late life can be reduced with annuities that pay until the named beneficiaries die. They may pay poorly or well, depending on the plan, but they eliminate the risk that bad investment decisions can leave someone broke.

Events That Can Dismantle a Retirement Plan

The problem that the best-laid plans can go terribly wrong pervades the entire process of planning retirement. You can develop a fine pension or RRSP, achieve substantial entitlements in government pension plans, and build up an impressive amount of capital through wise investments. But the plans you make can be derailed by unforeseen events.

When it comes to spending, you should establish a way of life that minimizes unexpected and large bills. The method is this: Anticipate and control expenses before they happen. You can buy critical illness insurance and supplemental health insurance for doctor and dentist bills, ambulance services, and drugs— depending on the province you live in. If you decide to buy a condo, ensure that there is already a substantial repair fund in place and that your co-owners are not so affluent that they may spend money and raise fees enough to harm your budget. If you have a house, manage upkeep to avoid major expenses. Small repairs are often less costly than repairs deferred until breakdowns happen. If you have a car, keep it well maintained. Some vehicles are famous for the high cost of parts and maintenance. Check it out before you buy a brand with service charges high enough to choke a tycoon. This is a strategic form of cost anticipation. After all, if your income is fixed or unlikely to grow much faster than inflation, it is vital to limit exposure to costs that can reduce discretionary income for other things.

Some of the largest cost issues arise in divorce or bankruptcy either before or after retirement. A planned pre-tax retirement income of $100,000 a year allows for a lot of good living, especially if your house is paid for, the kids have finished their degrees, and your life insurance is paid up. Cut that down to $50,000 before tax and divert some of that money to rent to replace a house lost to divorce and life is far less sweet.

Debt can also be a retirement wrecker. If a loan is affordable at 6 percent a year and interest rates double, the debt can threaten your financial security. No wonder retirements are more secure when all debts are paid.

The loans that should be paid off begin with debts at high interest rates such as sums owing on retailers' own credit cards, which can carry rates as high as 36 percent per year or more, debts due to universal charge cards like Visa or MasterCard that may carry rates of 20 percent per year, and unsecured signature loans and various student loans that may have been incurred by children. As each loan is paid off, cash flow is liberated to pay down other loans. When all loans have been paid, you are immune from rising interest rates.

Some retirees move offshore for a variety of reasons that may include living well at low cost. In other cases, the motive is escape from creditors. Running away from debts can be done, but the costs may be high. Canada imposes a departure tax on accrued but unrealized capital gains. In practice, you must tally all gains on taxable accounts (but not RRSPs) and deem them sold. The tax has to be paid as of the date of departure on the last return you file. Running away from creditors, including perhaps the Canada Revenue Agency, has another cost. It can become difficult to return to Canada to see friends and family. Life in tax havens such as the Caymans is costly. Anyone who seriously contemplates life in exile should include the costs of replacing provincial health insurance plans, the cost of lawyers to make this work, the potential problems of dealing with authorities in countries that may or may not have tax treaties with Canada, and much more.

You can also become vulnerable to unexpected costs as the result of a long illness and hospitalization, even though much of the cost of medical care is publicly funded. It can happen if your investments collapse or if a child desperately needs and is given substantial financial assistance. It can happen if you are sued for an injury and a court awards damages that are not covered by a comprehensive homeowner or tenant policy. The potential for financial disaster in the years of retirement is vast, but there are measures, discussed below, that you can take to limit financial risk.

Anticipating Misfortune

As a matter of planning, some misfortunes can be anticipated and mitigated. Critical illness insurance will cover some of the costs of prolonged, costly sickness. You can reduce the odds of being cleaned out by a stock market collapse by raising the bond content of your portfolio. A return to high inflation can be cushioned by the purchase of Real Return Bonds (called Treasury Inflation Protected Securities in the United States), which increase their value and payouts as each country's Consumer Price Index rises. Protection from civil judgments can be achieved in many cases by purchasing life insurance policies and certain annuity contracts that can be structured to be immune from many (but not necessarily all) claims of creditors, provided that it is not done as a way to flee from a debt recovery action already underway. As well, as a result of amendments to the federal Bankruptcy and Insolvency Act, registered investments such as RRSPs are protected from claims of creditors in bankruptcies filed after July 7, 2008.

All this tends to be wisdom in a paradoxical future hindsight. These financial protections can work, but each can also flop. Inflation-linked bonds can drop in value if inflation declines. A critical illness insurance policy is a waste of money if you do not have to claim on it. In general, if you insure every risk imaginable, the result is likely to be a financially safe life lived in reduced circumstances.

The problem comes down to seeing ahead. The New York Yankees' star catcher and manager Yogi Berra is said to have quipped, "Predictions are hard to make, especially about the future." That's especially true when you are trying to prepare for the next 30 or perhaps 40 years of life in a retirement beginning somewhere between the ages of 55 and 65. It is not enough to plan an income— you must also plan for the expenses the income is supposed to cover.

Inflation Risk

Perhaps the greatest single risk to financial plans is the return of high inflation, the most democratic of all forms of monetary misfortune. Even at a moderate rate of 2.5 percent for the next 20 years, inflation will cut the purchasing power of that $100,000 per year income down to $60,270. At 3.5 percent annual inflation, the purchasing power of $100,000 after 20 years will be $49,395. In planning retirement, it is essential to invest at rates that at least equal a rate of inflation that one may reasonably expect. And with that said, there is really no absolutely reliable way to predict inflation more than a few years into the future.

If prices were to rise at double-digit rates, bond prices would collapse, as they did from 1973 to 1982 in what may have been the worst bond market in history. Investment-grade bonds and government bonds would be devastated. Stocks would tumble as soaring financing costs crushed corporate profits.

Can that happen again? One school of gold investing says that paper money is due to lose value. Fiat money, a term of derision for the paper currencies issued by most countries without backing by gold, could go the way of the German mark when it fell to one six-billionth of its 1914 value by October 1923. This is a worst-case scenario and it is pretty unlikely. But it could happen. In late 1998, the Russian ruble collapsed and the Thai baht imploded. Investors who hold bonds of nations that are serial defaulters are in much the same situation. Worthless money is much the same as no money. The lesson? There is always safety in diversifying one's assets and currencies.

QUESTION: Inflation can devastate the value of life insurance payouts, bond interest coupons, and fixed pension benefits. What can be done about it?

ANSWER: Diversify into many sectors. Commodity prices rise when there is inflation. Different countries have varying inflation rates. Spread your money across sectors and countries and you reduce your vulnerability to inflation.

Asset Protection Strategies

The question is how you should diversify. What should you anticipate in a future that can stretch out for three or four decades? It is obvious that the longer the period of prediction, the more hazy the view becomes. We can predict with a high level of certainty what price levels and interest rates will be in a week. In 10 years, it's anyone's guess.

Bond portfolio managers get paid handsome salaries for making long-term bets on interest rates for 10, 20, and even 30 years. But bond managers are different from you and me. A life insurance company can make fairly accurate guesses about what percentage of its risks, as they call the folks they insure, will die in 2032 and 2037. It knows what it has to pay each, so buying bonds to back the policies involves relatively little risk. The policies are sold and the insurance company is just covering its own exposure.

For the individual retiree or someone planning to retire, the risk is far greater. The growing popularity of retirement before age 65 may make it even harder to cover all the risks.

The ability of pension systems to support folks retiring early is declining. The dependency ratio—that is, the proportion of those 65 and over to others who remain in the labour force—is growing. According to the federal Department of Finance, the ratio of 65-and-overs to workers was 20 percent in 2005 and will rise to 40 percent in 2030 and 44 percent in 2050. That is not as bad as the dependency ratio of Italy, where early retirement is even more popular. In that country, the 30 percent ratio in 2005 is due to rise to 68 percent in 2050. In Japan, where the birth rate has plummeted to below the replacement rate for the population, the dependency ratio, 30 percent in 2005, is expected to rise to 72 percent in 2050. Only the United States among all G-7 nations will escape the problem. Its dependency ratio, 19 percent in 2005, will peak at 32 percent in 2050.[5] The transition from sustainable social benefits to unsustainable benefits will accelerate in 2011 when the baby boomers, those people born after the end of World War II, begin to retire. Those born in 1946 will be 65 in that year. And it is only three years away as I write this chapter.

As the dependency ratio rises, the tax system will find it ever harder to maintain pensions and medical benefits for retirees. There will be more retirees and fewer workers to support them. According to Norma Kozhaya, a Quebec-based economist who prepared a report on the problem for the Montreal Economic

Institute in June 2007, "This will result in lower growth of tax revenues just as requirements and spending levels go up, especially in health care."[6]

The cure for the problem is to get more people paying taxes. That could be done by boosting the reward for working longer. Currently, the Canada and Quebec Pension Plans increase by 0.5 percent the benefits for each month after age 65 that benefits begin up to age 70, when the total bonus is 30 percent of the basic pension available at age 65. The Kozhaya report recommends that the bonus rise to 0.7 percent per month. As well, the penalty for retiring before age 65, which is a reduction of 0.5 percent per month for each month prior to age 65 at which benefits begin, could be increased. For example, a person retiring at age 60 would then receive CPP or QPP benefits that are cut by 0.7 percent per month for each month prior to age 65 at which benefits begin. The result of delaying receiving the CPP until 70 would be an effective bonus of 12 months per year times 5 years times 0.7 percent or a 42 percent boost in payments per year for waiting until age 70 to retire. Looked at from the point of view of a person considering early application for CPP/QPP benefits, the penalty for retirement at age 60 would be a 42 percent cut in age 65 benefits. At present, the bonus and penalty work out to 30 percent at ages 70 and 60, respectively. The Chief Actuary of Canada has said that the present system is unfair to people who retire later and too generous to those who retire early.[7]

Public pension authorities are likely to adjust the influences to early retirement to make them less attractive. The alternative would be the politically undesirable step of raising taxes to cover the costs of early retirement by millions of boomers.

The average retirement age in Canada in 2007 was 61.5.[8] Some private pension plans have bridge benefits, effectively a bonus, that brings early retirement income up to a level comparable to what the recipient would receive at age 65. Combined with progressive tax rates that take less when one earns less, workers may find themselves better off retiring early than continuing to work.[9] The benefit to the individual who has a workable retirement plan that can function securely before an age 65 commencement is obvious. The burden on the public pension system from encouraging people to leave the labour force and reduce their contributions to pension systems and, indeed, to the general revenues of government is also apparent.

Market Cycles and Retirement

The planning dilemma posed by retirement only grows more severe as the intended date of retirement is moved farther away. What is hard to foresee in ten years is almost impossible to predict at 30 or even 40 years. Add to that the very human tendency to assume that what is will be. Do you plan for high inflation as it existed in 1980, sluggish stock prices as they existed in the 1970s, low interest rates as they existed in 2004, or what seems to be an endless boom in commodity prices and prices of commodities producers as exists today?

The answer is none of the above. When trends move far from their historical averages, there are pressures that bring them back to the long-term mean. The commodities boom underway as I write this chapter will not last forever, just as interest rates could not stay depressed at very low single digits, as they were in 2004. So you must plan for what amounts to a normalized economic world but cover your bets just in case, at the time of retirement, the world is going the wrong way.

Let me give an example. In 2004, interest rates in the United States and Canada were at historical lows. It was a good time to take out a mortgage on a house and a terrible time to buy an annuity, which is really a life insurance policy running backward. Annuities typically guarantee to pay the annuitant a monthly sum for his or her life. The money used to buy the annuity winds up in government bonds. Low interest rates mean that annuities pay a pittance compared to what they pay when interest rates are high. A person who bought an annuity in 2004 was the victim of a phase of the interest rate cycle.

Someone who bought an annuity in 1982, when interest rates were 15 percent on long bonds, was in the very opposite situation. Annuity contracts purchased in 1982 were golden, as were investment-grade bonds that generated huge capital gains as interest rates fell and made existing bonds with relatively high fixed interest rates very valuable.

Can you foretell the future? Not accurately, of course. But you can adopt strategies that allow options for adapting to changing times. A good example is the Registered Retirement Income Fund option of paying out the value of an RRSP. It allows for the continuation of RRSP investments in virtually any asset class, including corporations that own or manage real estate and commodities. Real estate other than one's home purchased through the Home Buyer's Plan and commodities are excluded from RRSPs if they lack corporate shells. Flexible investment plans allow for progressive reduction of risk as one ages by shifts from stocks to bonds.

The problem in structuring any investment plan is what one may call the value horizon. An investor at the age of 20 may have a horizon of 65 years—that is, he can expect to live to age 85. He can accept losses with the assurance that he has time to make them up. The investor who is 80 and infirm may have only a few years to make up losses. A sensible investment plan has to take life expectancy into consideration. Indeed, any plan that is designed to sustain a certain way of life has to be structured to provide a minimum income regardless of the state of the economy or capital markets. If it does not, then the elderly investor may find it necessary to slash expenditures if income or assets fall.

The alternative to spending less is, obviously, to increase one's cash flow. It may become easier than ever, for by 2016, young people entering the labour force will no longer be numerous enough to replace those retiring and retired. The problem of a rising ratio of retired persons dependent on ever fewer workers will be embedded in two factors: 1) a birth rate that will give 1.5 children to each woman—obviously less than the two required to replace the parents and 2) increasing life expectancy. Immigration will not solve the problem, for, as the Toronto *Globe and Mail* pointed out on July 18, 2007, in a story about the changing population structure of Canada, the average age of immigrants is 30, an age past the prime years of reproduction.

By 2017, there will be more older people leaving the labour force than younger ones entering it. Compulsory retirement, already an outmoded model for the labour force, will become a relic of a time when baby boomers were entering the labour force in large numbers. Senior citizens in good health will have abundant work opportunities. Some of those openings will be replacing the young in entry-level jobs. But seniors will be in a job market quite receptive to them.[10]

There is a fundamental problem of working beyond the customary or perhaps the formerly customary age of 65. While life expectancy is growing, health expectancy is lagging. The result is that although many more people will make it to their nineties or even become centenarians, many will not be well enough to work. Of course, the probability of being in poor health grows with age. In the end, the fear that one will not have enough money to live on remains vivid and valid. The increase in life span only lengthens the prospective period of possible insolvency.

How Financial Planners See Retirement

The earlier you retire and the more completely you retire, the greater the odds of winding up poor at the end of life. Financial planners who add five years to the conventional life expectancy of 77 for men and 82 for women and then assume in their calculations that their clients should exhaust their financial assets by the respective dates are not leaving much room for error. The younger the age at which a plan is made, the more chance there is that medical advances will extend life and therefore financial jeopardy. Therefore, working longer than 65 can thus prop up financial plans that have not sufficiently anticipated long life.

The problems of planning are only partly embedded in life expectancy. There is also the conundrum of what assets to buy. In financial analysis, there are five traditional asset classes: stocks, bonds, real estate, cash, and commodities. In fact, there are more asset classes, for investment bankers have been amazingly creative in engineering exotic and even bizarre bets on climate and weather, currency variations, and even the outcome of elections. We will stick to the traditional five, however. Each asset class has its day. Canadian real estate and stocks have done well since the end of the tech bubble in 2002, government bonds did well from 1982 to 2002, and cash was king from 1973 to 1982. One could not see much future in base metals or fertilizer during the tech boom, but since 2005, those commodities have been among the hottest assets in the world. The future is fog. The wisdom of keeping some assets in each basket is undeniable. The problem is how to weight those baskets.

Several years ago, while writing my Financial Facelift column for the *Globe and Mail*, I came across the sad case of a family whose fortune had been devastated by an expertly drafted condition in a will. The testator instructed his executors to establish a trust that would invest in nothing but 90-day U.S. Treasury bills. The will was drawn up in 1980 when interest rates were rising. Stocks were in trouble, bonds were being slaughtered, and cash—held in the form of 90-day Treasury bills—was the best thing going. You could get 1 percent per month on Treasury bills with no risk of loss. The testator decided in the mood of the moment that nothing would ever beat a Treasury bill. His heirs wound up with returns of a few percent a year after trustees' fees took 4 percent per year off the nominal 6 percent average annual return in the period from his death in 1982 to a court hearing to modify the will in 1996. Had beneficiaries been allowed to hold a diversified portfolio of stocks, they would have been able to get an average annual return of 14 percent per year in the period from 1982 to 2001.[11]

The problem returns to the difficulty of seeing what is ahead. We do not know which asset classes will be best in five or ten years. Rather than try to boost returns by making long-term commitments to 20- or 30-year bonds that may generate better returns than shorter term bonds under some conditions, or buying risky stocks on the notion that return is proportional to risk (it is, but it may take decades to work out), you should ask a different and vital question: What set of investments and expense projections are least likely to leave you insolvent in 10 or 20 or 30 years?

Planning Strategies

It is not enough to stay in cash. Cash depreciates with inflation and, over a course of many years, money held in banknotes or in savings accounts that pay less than inflation on an after-tax basis are sure to suffer deep cuts to purchasing power.

As well, cash held in accounts that are not tax deferred, such as RRSPs, can generate interest that is taxable at peak rates. Cash is many things. It is liquid, it can be safe when held in government-guaranteed bank accounts, and it has no short-term risk of loss. But it is wrong as a long-term asset.

It is also wrong to do the opposite, that is, invest in assets that generate no income. Stocks of small companies that need to retain all their income, junk bonds that pay high rates of interest but that have credit ratings indicating they will probably default within five or ten years, and commodity funds that cite recent performance but do not disclose the long history of boom and bust in metals and minerals are all wrong as major holdings for retirement assets. Having a small percentage of one's money in such assets is probably harmless, but such investments are speculative and the returns often not much different than going to Vegas.

The majority of one's money should be in dividend-paying stocks or other assets that may rise in value or that have no risk of default—which is the virtue of government bonds—or that provide both value in use, as one's house or condo does, and potential value in exchange if they are sold at a profit. There is plenty of upside in each of these assets and relatively little downside when you compare them to stocks of startup companies, junk bonds, and investments in commodities that may be hot one day and comatose the next. For the retired investor and for those close to terminating employment as a source of income, conservative strategies are not merely safe, they are essential.

The concept of security in asset selection is to hedge one's bets by selecting assets that do more than one thing. Thus a stock with a strong and rising dividend is intrinsically more secure than a stock with no dividend. Should the dividend-paying stock's market price fall, the dividend will help make it up and, indeed, will tend to limit how far the stock may fall. A convertible bond has exposure to both bond interest rates and stock prices. One may shore up the other, though both drivers can also sink the bond if interest rates soar, making the company pay more for borrowed funds and reducing the value of its outstanding bonds. Above all, you should recall the maxim that it is wrong to put too many eggs in one basket. Risk is present in every act and, for that matter, every inaction.

The virtues of diversification have been proven with a great deal of fancy math by the same people who invented a hedge fund, Long-Term Capital Management. Bond trading was run by a legendary Wall Street bond trader with help from a couple of Nobel Prize–winning economists. Their trading formulas did not quite mesh with reality, and the insolvency of a reported US$1.2 trillion threatened the world's financial system. The U.S. Federal Reserve and tycoon Warren Buffett, as well as many banks, bailed out LTCM and saved the world. The lesson: Beware fund managers who come bearing gifts of esoteric theory.

Stick to Common Sense

It is good sense to build up a portfolio of assets not closely linked and that march to different drummers. Then you have both a portfolio that resists plunging in value when any one market drops and a means of tapping any market in the portfolio that is doing well. It would be wonderful if we could target just the markets that are going to do well, but it is almost impossible. A great financier was asked long ago, "What stocks should I buy?" He answered, "Buy the ones that are going up." "But what if they don't go up?"

asked the would-be investor. "Then don't buy them," came the great man's reply.

There is truth in this quote, for most of the big gains in stocks and bonds are the ones that few see coming. After all, if a major move up is obvious, investors will buy into it and raise the price of the stock. By the time that an anticipated event has happened, the stock will already have risen in price. So following the herd tends not to be a winning strategy. In the end, some of the best investors are the most cautious, sticking to what they know, studying companies and trends, and never betting too much on any one play. This is, of course, no way to get rich quick, but it is also not a way to get poor suddenly. In investing, the race often really does go to the tortoise. A wise one, to be sure.

I have been asked many times what is the best investment. The answer I give is one word: education. Capital markets—stocks and bonds, real estate, commodities, and so on—are a fascinating field. The more you learn, the less likely you are to be gulled by come-ons such as claims for amazing investments that pay 20 percent per month or 50 percent a year. There is no need to learn to pick your own stocks. Investment managers can handle the tasks, but it is vital to know how to judge managers.

It is also vital to know how to judge proposed deals. The question is not only whether they perform well, but whether they are worth the fees charged, whether a portfolio of funds is appropriate to one's needs, and whether rewards are worth risks taken. Financial planners may have the capacity to understand these vital issues, but then you need to be able to judge the planners. This is no easy task when some planners cover their mistakes with amiable patter. There can be substance to the patter, for one of the investor's greatest challenges is to be patient. In the long run, stocks and real estate rise in price. Bonds rise to or decline to their face value by maturity. And commodity prices reflect their value in world trade or industrial processes, in feeding people or growing things, or, as in the case of gold, in storing value.

At the end of *When Can I Retire?* you will find a list of books that can help you judge investments and investment managers. As a matter of sheer interest, the quest can be absorbing. Considering that this is a field that can be immensely profitable and that you can learn to pick better managers and get higher or perhaps more secure returns, study is worthwhile.[12]

Chapter Summary

Retirement has come to mean a period at the end of a career, when living costs are financed in part by government pensions as well as private savings. Today, with large numbers of people able to get to retirement age, the costs governments bear are large. There is widespread fear that our prosperous life in middle age will turn into poverty in old age. The risk of poverty can be reduced by diversifying your investments. With the tools provided in *When Can I Retire?*, it is possible to reduce the odds of becoming poor in the later years of life and, indeed, to increase the odds of being well off.

Chapter 2

The Big Gamble: Setting Up a Retirement Plan

The decision to retire is one of the biggest gambles that any of us will make in our lives. The choice to reduce income or stop earning income altogether and to rely on pensions from government or personal savings, along with the assumption that one's costs are predictable for a period of what may turn out to be decades, is a very big bet. If it turns out badly, it may not be possible to correct the mistake. Compulsory retirement may be dying a deserved death, but the reality of the job market is that it is hard to begin a new career at 55 or 65 or 75.

Retirement is inevitable—indeed, it eventually becomes a physical reality for most people who do not succumb to death or disability. But framing that retirement and planning it is not without challenges. Many of the things we want to predict are really not readily knowable. In the void of knowledge about the future, we still have to make fundamental decisions that can last for life and even into the lives of our heirs. Moreover, the farther in the future that any financial plan is set to begin, the greater is the intrinsic risk that it may fail to anticipate the future correctly.

The problem of estimating the "right" retirement year and then calculating budgets and incomes for the remaining years of life is that the process is about both rational pencil work and irrational desires to be free to travel or play golf, fish, etc. The notion of years of golfing is less than rational because it is very hard to put a number on the pleasure that comes from it. Therefore, we have to assume that every use of money produces equal amounts of satisfaction. Thus $5 spent on a bottle of table wine produces the same pleasure or satisfaction as $5 spent on a cocktail or a 30-minute session at a driving range. And that is clearly not so. The old saying that one man's meat is another's poison goes to the heart of financial planning. Every plan has to be personal. Investment and cash flow formulas can never do more than extend present values into the future. They can never tell you how to live.

This chapter is an overview of the risks one faces as the years of life ahead grow shorter. The risks inherent in a stock market meltdown of the kind that occurred in 2007 and 2008 are more profound when one is older, for there is less time to recover. Likewise, the consequences of error in planning your life ahead grow more serious if you make an error. The odds of making mistakes do not necessarily change, but their consequences do. Nevertheless, we have to work within these parameters, and so we assume that a buck is a buck no matter how it is spent.

The Uncertainties of Retirement

We have to break down the unknowns in planning retirement so that they can be addressed in making financial scenarios and plans.

Value of assets. What will you be worth on the day you retire? If, on the day you plan to buy an annuity or perhaps to close a deal on a new, smaller home, the stock market or any other fluctuating asset market is in a severe retreat, your plans can be knocked askew.

Predictability of returns from savings and investments. This is perhaps the greatest of the unknowns. It is possible for returns to be low or negative for periods of many years. People who sell stocks and bonds like to quote the superior long-run returns of stocks in comparison to bonds and cash. Indeed, over periods of several decades, stocks have produced twice the returns of bonds and about four times the returns of cash equivalents like Treasury bills. Spreading your money around reduces the chances of portfolio collapse, for there is no foolproof system beyond the old adage that you should not put all your eggs in one basket.

Health and costs. Provincial health insurance, even with backing from private health insurance, is never complete. Costly drugs for treatment for grave diseases tend not to be covered by private medical plans. Some people are able to lobby for special consideration and some get it. The idea that, if you are seriously ill, insurance will pay any and all costs is speculative, to say the least.[1] You may want or need to go to an alternative health care provider in the United States—say the Mayo Clinic or the Cleveland Clinic, both renowned for their work. The costs of these alternatives can be astronomical.

Reliability of income. Rumours persist that the Canada Pension Plan and the Quebec Pension Plan will run out of cash. Reports from actuaries say the opposite. This is not an issue that should be troubling. But corporate pension plans are another issue. Many in the United States have failed, and others in Canada have had to cut cost of living indexation to inflation in order to remain solvent.

The state of your life. Much will depend on whether you have planned an orderly retirement and have a partner to share the years after work. In the years leading up to retirement, it's wise to be sure your capital goods—house and car, perhaps cottage and boat—are in good order. Heavy capital expenses should come in the working years, not after.

The state of the world. If there is a law of history, it is that things change. Good neighbourhoods go bad. Cottages perched on beaches near shorelines fall into the water as coastlines erode. The last century provided awful demonstrations of what happens when madmen take over nations. Hitler and Stalin used genocide as state policy. In the 21st century some Pacific islands may disappear if the oceans rise from global warming. The point of all this is not to try to predict geology or major events in history, but to keep your options open.

Your state of mind about retirement. This is perhaps the hardest factor to estimate. If you enter retirement with regret and even anticipation of tough times to come, the years will pass slowly and painfully. On the other hand, if years of playing tennis or golf, travelling, or visiting your children are appealing, then the future can be attractive and sensible. The value of creating a desirable retirement structure is obvious.

The problems of foreseeing the future and planning for what can be foretold are growing. A century ago, life expectancy was far shorter than it is today. Those fortunate enough to have savings or defined benefit pensions did not have to worry about what might lie 30 years ahead. Today, a long-range outlook has to be part of the concern of each retiree. Those who think they can retire early at age 55 or even 45 have even more to be concerned about. Women, in particular, may be less than halfway through their lives at the age of 40.

Employability. This is a vital issue, for, according to Statistics Canada, people aged 55 to 64 made up 16.9 percent of the total workforce in 2006 and that could be 20 percent in 2016. "With workers generally leaving the workforce between the ages of 55 and 64, Canada has never had so many people close to retirement," said Statistics Canada.[2] Many will leave, but with relatively fewer workers below age 55 to 64 in the labour force in comparison to those 55 and older, the potential opportunities for seniors to remain employed are growing. That said, whether one wishes to work will remain a personal decision based on budget and retirees' tastes for travel, tennis, or any other form of leisure.

Inflation. A few examples of what can happen in just 30 years show the problems that have to be confronted when you're planning for far in the future.

- In 1960, $2,000 would buy a new compact car, you could see Europe on $5 per day, and a bottle of Coke could be had at vending machines for 10 cents. In 1990, $2,000 would buy only a well-used car. Travel in Europe was possible on $75 per day. A Coke cost $1 at most vending machines.
- In 1970, $125,000 would buy a sound house in a Toronto suburb like Don Mills. Paperback novels cost 35 cents. Ten dollars bought a good dinner at an upscale restaurant. By 2000, the house was $1.25 million, dinner was $90, and the paperback novel was $6.95.

- In 1980, a man's suit at a fine tailor shop cost $400. A pair of women's shoes from a posh store would top out at $300. By 2010, the man's suit will easily cost $2,000, with exquisite fabrics pushing the price to $5,000. That pair of women's shoes could be $1,500.

QUESTION: Setting up retirement plans far into the future presents a question of returns and certainty of fees. What can you do to reduce the chance that years of fees will eat up the variable fortunes of investments?

ANSWER: Diversify into several asset classes, such as bonds and stocks, perhaps life insurance or real estate, watch the fees charged by mutual funds, and review the performance of your assets at least once a year to ensure the fees you pay are generating the results you want. You may have to allow for downturns in various markets, but over time, it is vital that you get what you are paying for. After all, a 2 percent annual management or administration fee will take 40 percent of your assets in 20 years. If management has added at least 2 percent on average year after year to the return of a benchmark such as the S&P/TSX Total Return Index, then the fees may be worthwhile.

The Value of Diversification

A simple rule of thumb shows the effects of inflation. It uses a traditional and very workable little formula based on the number 72. It turns out that when you divide 72 by some interest rate—any interest rate you like—you can get the number of years that it takes for money to double. For example, in a simple case, if interest rates are 12 percent per year, then if you divide 72 by 12, you find that a sum of money, any sum at all, will double in 6 years. It works just as well with inflation. Take the number 72 and divide it by an estimate for the rate of inflation—bond strategists today consider that the long-range rate of inflation is 2.5 to 3.0 percent per year. For simplicity, let's use 3 percent: 72 divided by 3 is 24. That is the number of years it will take for prices to double if inflation is running at 3 percent per year. Each quarter century, prices will double. To ensure that you have sufficient spending power after tax, you probably need to earn 5 percent to keep up with that 3 percent rate of inflation. That's because you have to earn $5 to keep $3 as inflation compensation if you are in a common 40 percent tax bracket.

Stocks historically have returned 8 percent per year, bonds 4 percent, and cash and short-term Treasury bills 3 percent. So a portfolio of stocks will double in value every nine years, bonds will keep pace with inflation before tax and barely pace it after tax, and cash and cash equivalents, which at best earn only a return equal to the rate of inflation before tax, will eventually leave you broke, having failed to keep up with inflation.

The solution to controlling risk is to have some of each. Stocks can be as much as 75 percent of the portfolio of a person under 25 and as little as 10 percent of the portfolio of a person at age 90. The remainder should be bonds or cash or cash equivalents, depending on the level of interest rates and the outlook for fixed income assets. Remember that we are talking about an average retirement with what can be considered average risks and exposure to average costs. There is much debate as to whether costs of living rise in retirement or decline—after all, you will have paid off a house mortgage, put the kids through school, and built up savings.

Whether costs go up or down is often up to individuals and their chosen way of life.

In the following analysis of costs, which is only a preliminary step, we'll see that cost variation or, if you like, cost uncertainty is a function of choice. It is controllable within limits, though each choice bears costs of its own.

In spite of the problems of foretelling the future, it has to be done. One solution is to set retirement not as a goal, but as a series of steps. You may choose to retire at 60 and expect 10 years of travel and vigorous pastimes. Then another 10 years of less activity and finally 10 years when you will be less mobile and perhaps require some measure of help to get through the day. Such a plan allows for diminishing expenditures and is workable within broad limits. Whatever plan you choose, it is essential to leave ample "wiggle room." In practice, this means not just getting ends to meet, but building in a generous cushion of extra cash flow or extra wealth to allow for the unexpected—such as living a long and rich life. How much more that extra cash flow should be is uncertain, though it will vary with every case. Perhaps 10 percent more cash flow and 10 percent more savings than you think you need at age 65. The longer the plan, the greater the need for a cushion to soften the blows of the unexpected. At age 75, the cushion might be 8 percent, at 85, 5 percent.

Timing Retirement

Financial Facelift, my weekly feature for personal finance at the *Globe and Mail*, gets a huge amount of mail from readers who want to retire before age 65. The most popular idea seems to be retirement at age 55. This is the effect in part of a marketing program by London Life that has generated substantial business on the theory that early retirement is achievable by ordinary folks who have the wisdom to buy certain financial products.

The notion of retirement at age 55 has become what amounts to a generic concept, a belief that with some fiddling with investments, it can be done. In reality, it is not attainable for most folks. Gordon Pape, a veteran Canadian personal finance authority, said, "Most Canadians fail to grasp [that] early retirement is a pipe dream."[3]

Time creates two very distinct problems in estimating how much money one needs to retire. The first is, of course, the length of the retirement period covered. The second is the consequence of retiring early, that is, less time to save for whatever retirement period is chosen.

Assume that a person at age 45 works for another 20 years, putting $10,000 per year to her RRSP and generating a pre-inflation return of 7 percent per year. She would have $438,652 by the time she is 65. Adjusted for 3 percent average annual inflation, she would have $305,632.

On the same assumptions, what happens if our person retires at age 55 and stops contributing to her RRSP? She would have $147,836 before inflation adjustments or $124,864 after adjustment for inflation running at an average annual rate of 3 percent.

The cost of retiring at age 55 is clearly very large. In this case, the reduction in RRSP assets is 67 percent of what the individual could have by working to age 65.

Less money available at retirement translates to a riskier retirement. Every spending decision will have a potentially larger effect on assets because, of course, one will have fewer assets. Thus the $10,000 vacation will be harder to finance and a larger strike against capital for the person who retires at age 55 as compared to one who retires at age 65.

Risk is merely theoretical until it turns into actual dollars and cents. At that time, what was merely speculation turns into a reality check of what can be and what cannot, what is feasible now but may cripple the retirement plan in future.

QUESTION: Can you make a plan for a retirement 20 years away that may last 40 years?

ANSWER: You can, but you need to diversify assets and avoid getting locked into assets that will be devastated by inflation. Plan for flexibility and to maintain choice. Plan as well to have more income or wealth than you think you need. This is the safety belt that will protect your retirement if costs rise unexpectedly or income declines.

Large Potential Retirement Expenditures

First and foremost, the greatest expense will be shelter. If the mortgage on your principal residence is paid or small, there's no problem. If it is large or if you plan to buy a vacation property, the problem of housing can be substantial. Along with the capital cost or mortgage, you have to estimate such things as upkeep and property taxes and, for condos, strata fees or common area costs. The more you have to pay for shelter and, if you have a mortgage, the more debt you have, then the greater is the risk you carry. For example, if you have a two-income or two-pension family and one person dies, the greater will be the chance that the survivor's cost of living will rise. The survivor will still have the fixed costs of shelter and one less income to use to pay them. As well, if the mortgage outstanding is exposed to changing interest rates, a rise in the mortgage rates could be crippling.

Next comes social spending. With more time on your hands, you'll need to create activities that fill the hours you spent at your job. Stereotypically, people spend more time on golf or bridge, more time on cruises, more time visiting friends and children.

Taxes rise with income and with expenditure. Retirement may mean a lower income and thus lower income taxes, but taxes on consumption rise with spending. And they do so at an exponential rate. Just as cost of living data track costs on a compound basis, tax gains are calculated on the existing rate. If taxes increase at just 3 percent per year, then after a decade they will be 34 percent higher than at the beginning of the calculation period.

Medical, dental, and drug expenses may be substantial, even with provincial health care plans. You may decide to purchase critical illness insurance and upgrade medical insurance policies to cover additional drug costs. You will find a good deal of variability in price and structure, but, as a typical example, one major vendor sells coverage for a 55-year-old male non-smoker for $99 per month. The policies are restricted to defined diseases such as heart attack and cancer and some require that you survive at least a month after diagnosis.

Discretionary spending on home renovations may rise. You may want to buy a large recreational vehicle or a second home. Neither of these possibilities can be part of a general budget, but each illustrates the potential for additional spending in retirement. Some of this spending may be less than pre-retirement spending when you were paying a mortgage and saving up for children. But for each child who finishes university, there may be a grandchild for whom you want to contribute to a Registered Education Savings Plan.

A critical variable in estimating spending is age. Spending may rise when retirement begins, then decline as you settle into old age. The last rooms of one's life are likely to be small and living in them is likely to be economical.

The idea that we need less space and perhaps fewer things as life heads toward its conclusion is behind the notion that you can boost your retirement income in later years by downsizing your house or moving to a less expensive condo or rental unit. That is true and, if you sell a principal residence, there will be no tax on the capital gain.

On the other hand, the psychological implication of being forced to sell your house in order to survive for another few years is unattractive. It is tinged with the idea of being pushed into poverty. It has negative repercussions. And so it should be part of a planning process only when it is understood as acceptable, as it may be if the new quarters are more appropriate to your life in retirement. Access to work, schools, and playgrounds—things that mattered when, as parents, we were concerned with children—are likely to be less important and issues such as easier housekeeping become more appealing. The new quarters may be in adult-only communities or in buildings that offer assisted living. Or perhaps you will make an even greater move and live in Europe for its culture or the tropics for the weather. Downsizing makes sense when the cost of sale is balanced by genuine gains.

The Economic Consequence of a More Economical Life

Downsizing becomes more than a matter of choosing ski slopes or palms when your identity seems attached to your residence. Farmers who are forced to sell for lack of children to take over the business or who have to sell to be closer to medical care undergo a wrenching change of life. They are not alone. When a small business has been a way of life for many decades or even the better part of a century, selling is only the first step in the reorganization of a way of life. An economic gain on the sale of the business may be offset by new costs incurred in adapting to living in the city or to finding ways to fill the hours that the business required.

Downsizing from a house to an assisted living situation or a nursing home can be wrenching both in the psychological costs of giving up familiar and loved furniture and the possessions of a lifetime and in the costs that go along with institutional living with substantial personal assistance. As we age, our mobility decreases. We may no longer be able to drive and may have to use public transport or taxis. The costs of such services may be higher or lower than the costs of operating a car, but the trauma of losing a large measure of independence is undeniable.

There is another dimension to psychological costs—togetherness and singleness. The old adage that two can live more cheaply than one is correct if the assumption is that one just totals up costs and divides by two. Yet there is another value in singleness and togetherness that goes beyond arithmetic.

Quality of life issues often tilt on a fulcrum of singleness or togetherness. If you are married or in a similar living arrangement, the death or departure of a spouse or partner can trigger many costs from funeral arrangements, if that is the event in question, to separation costs if that is involved. You can plan for funeral expenses via life insurance or pre-paid burial arrangements. Separation costs are much harder to plan for. At the worst, a separation can reduce your standard of living drastically. Loss of home, the cost of moving, the psychological toll of having your life picked apart, and division of pensions and assets impose a heavy cost on your well-being. This book is no place for a discussion of the mechanics of separation or of asset protection. It is appropriate, however, to suggest that if separation is foreseeable, it is correct to take advice and act in accord with counsel. The advice may include personal assistance from friends or professionals, for becoming single late in life may produce personal and financial shocks from which it is hard to recover.

On a strictly financial basis, the costs of living apart or together can be estimated. Together may mean two incomes or two sets of pensions with costs that are only slightly higher for two than for one. This is a situation in which standards of living may improve. The costs of living apart are the opposite: fairly constant costs of maintaining a house or renting an apartment but a severe reduction in pension income.

If a change in the circumstances of living is in the offing, it is easy to do a spreadsheet in order to compare the income and expense of either arrangement. If you have the good fortune to be saving a good deal of your income, then a change of arrangement may not have an immediate impact on your living standard. If savings are slim and costs are high in relation to income, the risks of mortality or separation should be factored into the future.

And so we return to the issue of time, which is diminishing for all of us but at a faster pace for the elderly. At age 60, men have an average 20.36 years of life ahead, women 23.53 years. At 75, there is a drop to 10.24 years for men and 12.29 years for women. At age 80, the numbers tumble to 7.62 years for men and 9.22 for women.[4]

This recitation of mortality figures should not obscure the salient point of every average: Half of those in each group will live longer than average. You can improve the odds of being a survivor by sensible living. As a financial matter, the better your health and the longer your life expectancy, the greater is the need to be prudent in investments.

For each individual, the time remaining to restore an investment or to pay off a debt is diminishing. That single fact puts a premium on planning—that is, on getting your finances in order. And that means controlling the risks of making wrong decisions or of exposing yourself to costly errors. It is an obvious point, but one that has to be made: The problem is greater for women because, statistically, they have an appreciably longer life span than men.

Risk Management

There is a simple way to estimate your financial risks. Let's use an example. If you have $500,000 in assets including a $10,000 stock with a 75 percent chance of generating a loss, your portfolio value at risk of loss is $3/4 \times \$10,000$ divided by $500,000 or 1.5 percent. If you have a 25 percent chance of losing on a $100,000 investment in a $500,000 portfolio, your portfolio value at risk is 5 percent.

The example shows the virtue of diversification. Diversification is a principle that applies not just to investments, which you can measure relatively well, but to things like hobbies and friendships. The greater the risk of failure and the more of your assets you bet, the larger are the odds of catastrophe should the gamble fail. For everyone, prudence is its own reward. For the elderly, it is essential.

A full life, one with many activities, many opportunities, and many options, is likely to be more fulfilling than one in which everything devolves into one view or relationship. Over time, it is inevitable that you will shed many things in life, but slowing that process is more likely to produce fulfillment and good use of your money than a life in which you are rushed into the isolation that often comes with retirement.

Life is more than money, of course. But the people who are going to be the most free to enjoy life will be those who have no substantial debts and little or no exposure to the cost of rising interest rates. They will be people who have set their incomes in retirement to be adequate for their expenses and who have financial reserves for unexpected costs. After all, to go into retirement with high hopes and few means is an invitation to disaster.

Timing Your Retirement

Inevitably the question arises—when should I begin to plan my retirement? And what assets should I have?

"When" is a fluid concept. Vendors of financial products like life insurance and mutual funds suggest that age 21 is a good time to start. Their reasoning—the longer you have to accumulate, the more you will have. What they do not say is that more time means more fees for you to pay. For a person at 20 who may retire at 55, there are 35 years of mutual fund fees for these companies to reap. Recall the example in the Question and Answer box on page 28— fees can add up to a shocking amount of money to pay for performance that is not readily predictable and that is almost certain to lag relevant indices over such extended periods. Life insurance premiums for whole life policies are very low for people in their twenties. But the paid-up value of the insurance will be eroded by inflation. Thus the benefit of buying whole life with low premiums in one's twenties is substantially lost after 40 years as retirement begins.

You can, of course, use low-fee or even zero-fee financial products for retirement savings. Exchange-traded funds with management fees perhaps a tenth of those of managed mutual funds are likely to outperform their high-fee competitors over periods of 10 or more years. ETFs are bought and sold like stocks on exchanges and replicate almost any index you'd like, from the Dow Jones Industrial Average to Swiss pharmaceutical companies, large cap companies in Asia, and, of course, major Canadian stock indices. You can also buy and hold solid companies. For example, the growth potential of Royal Bank common is illustrated by its history. Shares of Canada's biggest bank traded at $50 in May 2008, 12.5 times their $4.00 price on July 1, 1988. That works out to an average annual compound gain of 13.5 percent per year. Add dividends that averaged about 4 percent for much of the period and you get an average annual compound return of 17.5 percent. If Royal Bank repeats that performance, then in 2028, its shares will be worth $6,250 each, though they will have likely split a few times in the interim. One suspects that the dividends may not rise as fast as the share price, but—in any event—two decades of future growth of the shares of Canada's largest bank could produce a rich reward for their holders.

As part of an investment program, there is every reason to buy some stocks and bonds or exchange-traded funds in your twenties. The potential appreciation is obviously huge. But detailed retirement planning can be delayed until you're in your thirties or even early forties. That's when you have a better idea of the responsibilities ahead. Perhaps you have a family to support or children to be put through university. Maybe you have a spouse to support or someone who will be supporting you. In mid-life there is less time to build a portfolio, but you can see more clearly into the future. That advantage is ample compensation for what may be a decade or two of inflation that goes with very early retirement planning. Moreover, the fees paid to conventional mutual funds for an extra decade of financial management can cripple portfolio gains. Rather than take a shotgun approach to retirement, it makes sense to aim for needs that come into focus as you reach and surpass middle age.

In the following chapters, we'll examine cost projections for retirement in a series of stages of life and then examine in detail the various pension programs that are available to support retirement. The goal is to achieve at least a balance, a cash flow equal to expenses and perhaps more than expenses to provide a cushion for illness or travel or unexpected expenses. Our examination won't assume that all assets should be consumed by the end of life for that involves predicting death, even if you assume that "life" will be the actuarial estimate for your age and gender plus five years. No one should go to the grave completely busted. That situation is evidence of shrewd planning, but it can also be an example of someone heading to death with a sharp pencil and nothing to leave to beneficiaries. Indeed, the fact that people who have amassed significant and durable financial assets wisely express their testamentary wishes through wills shows that common sense trumps a financial planning assumption. In the remainder of this book, we shall avoid the assumption of total exhaustion of assets.

Chapter Summary

The greater the time to retirement and in retirement, the harder it is to make accurate predictions. But once in retirement, the margin of error may decrease. The older one is, after all, the more limited is the choice of things to do. Living with a spouse or anyone else also cuts costs per person, for many overhead expenses are readily shareable. Indeed, it is somewhat easier for a middle-aged person to assess his or her risks and to make sensible plans for retirement than it is for someone who is very young and unsure of his or her future. For that reason, postponement of retirement planning to the thirties or early forties is acceptable. Taking out life insurance coverage at this stage may result in higher premiums but the inflation problem will be less severe. Whatever plan is devised, build in wiggle room—that means extra income and extra wealth. Achieve cash flow in excess of expenses and add a cushion for the unexpected. When you have that, you are ready to retire.

Chapter 3

The Decision Point

Retirement is becoming less mandatory and more voluntary, the result of the laws that regulate retirement changing from imposing external rules to allowing personal choice. Many companies use generous buyout plans and pension schemes that cease to reward employees after age 60 as a way of making it easy for older workers to leave their jobs. This kind of out-migration by age reduces the pension and health care costs that go along with having older and usually more expensive long-term workers. Yet the decision to retire is increasingly individual. Many people are lured into retirement by the notion of "Freedom 55," the name of London Life's hugely successful marketing program. These early retirees have been motivated to leave their conventional employment on the theory that they can afford retirement and will enjoy it.

According to a January 2005 retirement survey by AXA, a global insurance company, Americans—and by implication, Canadians—start saving for retirement in their mid-thirties and see 58 as the ideal retirement age.[1] In the AXA study of Canadian retirement, 63 was the age at which people intended to retire. That's not far from the conventional retirement age of 65, but the trend is to voluntary retirement. Of the 78 percent of Canadians who retire early, 66 percent say they did so voluntarily.[2] In comparison, only 59 percent of those who retire early do so voluntarily in the United States.[3]

The decision to leave your employer or a profession is a milestone in life. It's a turning point, for once a person of late middle age leaves his customary employment, it is hard to go back. The law makes all job applicants equal, but the reality is that employers don't want to train older workers. The payback period will be shorter, they say, ignoring the higher job mobility of younger workers. Employers with supplemental medical and dental plans also want to keep their premiums down. Older people do make more demands on the health care system. Employers are struggling to be rational in trying to manage the costs of fringe benefits.

We cannot say that retirement is a one-way street to the end of work, for many people who retire early will move to part-time employment or self-employment or change their jobs. They may go from doing a task to teaching it. Or from work in a plant to volunteer work that is entirely unpaid or that has some modest payments to cover designated costs. Yet with the exception of employees who retire with generous pension plans then return to work on contracts, retirement remains a path of leaving a familiar career or profession for something less well known.

Planning to retire is both a matter of mapping out cash flow and expenses for the future and a sort of wing and a prayer hope that what you know today will still be true and right tomorrow. The longer the planning period, the more that can go wrong, as we saw in the previous chapter: The person retiring at age 75 may need to get cash flow and expenses right for only a decade, but the person who wants to quit work at 55 may have three or more decades to anticipate.

Rational planning and our desire for security, especially after work ends and income is limited, suggest that retirement be delayed as long as possible. But there are things you can do to reduce uncertainty, especially the risk of running out of money.

Building Income Security

Own annuities that promise a fixed amount of money every month until your death and/or the death of your spouse.

Invest in common stocks of companies that have paid and raised their dividends for decades.

Be in a defined benefit pension plan with indexation set to follow increases in the Consumer Price Index.

Hold government bonds that have no default risk and a diversified portfolio of high-quality corporate bonds with very little default risk.

Own inflation-linked bonds that raise their payouts as the CPI rises.

Retirement may look like a promised land. But once you have arrived, it can look very different. Therefore, in assessing retirement plans at any age, it pays to consider the positive and negative aspects of not going to work in the morning.

Reasons Not to Retire

Lack of incentives. You will have no reason to get up in the morning. The curse of employment is the schedule that compels you to go to the office or factory at one hour and return home at another or adapt to swing shifts. That curse is also a blessing, for it creates a rhythm of life or a structure. It gets you going in the morning, measures out your day, and provides a place where you have associates or even friends. A job is a purpose, a focus, and a reward.

Aloneness. For some people, the alternative to going to work is isolation, either with a spouse who has perhaps never had more than a vacation's worth of the full-time presence of the other spouse or living alone entirely.

Indolence. The lack of motivation for getting up in the morning can lead to passivity. You might get up later and later in the day and what's left of the day somehow melts away with nothing really accomplished or enjoyed. With no reason to get up or structure to your day, you may find yourself moving from one grown child's couch to another grown child's couch. You may fall prey to the temptation to have a cocktail before dinner, then perhaps one before lunch, and then just to have cocktails. Alcoholism rises with loneliness, and the elderly are uniquely exposed to the risk. In a study of persons 60 to 94 years of age, 62 percent of the subjects were found to drink alcohol, and heavy drinking was reported in 13 percent of men and 2 percent of women. Overall, about 6 percent of older adults are considered heavy users of alcohol. Heavy drinking is defined as having more than two drinks per day.[4]

Loss of identity. You could experience a loss of the sense of who you are. Identity and work go together today as much as ever. Work is the connection between the person and society. You can have any number of other attributes—membership in various organizations, holder of academic distinctions, and so on—but who you are is what you do.

Giving up the connection to work can be a crippling loss for many people. As much as they may have hated a boss or a cramped office, a lousy plant cafeteria or even difficult colleagues, the job is an identity. It may come with perks, it may be glamorous or unpleasant, but it is their tether to the world.

When the job is gone, along with the business card, the title on the door, and the other badges of office, you become something like the professor emeritus. Except that for most jobs, there is no emeritus. You get the gold watch or the $10 bottle of wine, the coffee and cake sendoff and then, if you return to where you worked, you can become a curiosity. Your former colleagues will greet you and silently hope you don't make a habit of coming back. Indeed, without the company ID card, you may not even be able to get into the building you called your second home unless you sign in at the front desk, confirming your status as an outsider.

Creditors will learn that you are no longer employed. It becomes harder to get a loan, a credit card with a substantial limit, even some kinds of insurance. It becomes obvious that having a job was a good thing and an even better one if it was of long tenure.

Giving up your status. You will have to relinquish the perks of the job. There's hardly any work that has no fringe benefits through the employer or a related professional association. The bigger the paycheque, the more perks that seem to come with it. And the larger the group that is involved, the richer the benefits seem to be.

The reasons for this largesse have more to do with marketing than with merit, but you'll miss them when they are gone. However, merchants do offer discounts to seniors and, in the United States and parts of Europe, the magic age for qualification can be as low as 45 or 50. The savings such discounts offer, though, are unlikely to offset the benefits that come with employment.

Losing perks. As a financial matter, the fringe benefits of employment have a definite value. If your company has kept your notebook computer in good health, provided a dental plan, allowed you to use its special rates at hotels, and obtained travel vacation deals, you'll have to forage far and wide to replace such advantages. Most of the time, the really big perks can't be replaced. The reasons have everything to do with age and demography.

In a company with employees arrayed in an age pyramid from many young people at the bottom of the ladder and a few older employees at the top, health benefits for the most senior employees are subsidized by the young. The healthy, younger people who seldom visit the doctor are carrying older workers who are heavy users of services not covered by provincial health plans.

Loss of financial safety nets. When you give up the financial cushion of subsidy by the young, the costs of replacing those health benefits are bound to soar. How much depends on the benefits in question, your health, perhaps your partner's health if it's a joint plan, and your province of residence.

One of the most important fringe benefits of a job is almost priceless. Many employers offer group life insurance. It's plain term coverage customarily set at two times annual pay. In a group plan, the young subsidize the old. Selling costs are distributed among many insured persons. When you're 60 or older, the cost of term coverage soars and in many cases, you can't buy coverage at all.

You should price the costs of group life and supplemental health benefits. Pay stubs will probably show the cost of this benefit to you as an employee. When you start shopping for comparable coverage, you are likely to find that what comes at a nominal or small cost with the job costs thousands to replace. Some coverage, such as disability, which is very expensive to purchase in the private market, ceases to have meaning when you no longer work.

Lack of pension. Lots of people have little or no pension benefits from employment. The pensionless include mums who have returned to the labour force after decades of child rearing and have not worked long enough to qualify for substantial pensions, people who have been job-hoppers and never stayed long enough to build up pensions, employees of small firms that never set up pensions, the self-employed who have only sparse RRSPs, people who have been stripped of assets in divorces, and parents who spent their savings to provide for the care of a sick child in need of treatment not provided by the Canadian health care system. They have a strong incentive to work and save for as long as possible.

Cost of replacing job-related transportation and accommodation. One of the most valuable perks of being an employee is the company car. The private use of a car is a taxable benefit, but it is one that is phenomenally valuable to employees. Assume that your company provides a car with a lease cost to the company of $500 per month. If you use it for personal purposes half the time, then you have a $250 taxable benefit. Your cost of running the car will be your tax rate, say 40 percent, times $250 or $100 per month. That is your total cost for running the car, apart from gas and washes, insurance, and so forth.

If you plan to do consulting after your formal career, be sure to figure the costs of setting up that kind of business. What can seem a good plan may turn out to be a pipe dream. Replicating your office—renting space in a building, hiring an assistant, and hooking up computers to provide the conveniences you have had in your workplace—is costly, though many of these costs are tax-deductible.

Loss of camaraderie. Workplace relationships provide intangible benefits. Going to an office every day can lead to conversation, bonding, perhaps romance, and, of course, to occasional discord. We focus our lives on work, so it is natural that work-related connections are important in our lives. Without those bonds, life can become quite grim. Isolation and mortality go together. For the employee with a limited social circle, the social associations of work can be life-saving.

Depression is a handmaiden of loneliness. Those who are alone have more time to dwell on their situations, often in very negative ways. They may feel abandoned, that life has passed them by. In a study of the problem, psychiatrists Max L. Stek and colleagues at Leiden University's Medical Centre, a major teaching facility in the Netherlands, found that mortality risk attributable to depression in the presence of perceived loneliness was 2.1 times the normal risk in the population. To be old and alone is often to be depressed. The combination is deadly.[5]

There are cures to loneliness when one is old. Nursing homes create play times for their patients. Senior day care offers some solace. But for a person who has been active at work, being paid for his or her accomplishments, party games are an insult. To quit work and to wind up spending months or years in a game room is demeaning, to say the least. It is not a substitute for work and, seen in perspective, it is actually a pretty good reason to be depressed.

No compulsion to retire. Rules and laws compelling retirement are becoming obsolete and are swiftly being turfed out in recognition of the new reality that the economy needs seniors to stay at work. Ontario, Quebec, Manitoba, Alberta, Prince Edward Island, Nunavut, the Yukon, and the Northwest Territories have limited the reach of laws compelling retirement at given ages. Other provinces such as Nova Scotia allow compulsory retirement provided it is done in a prescribed manner. The federal government allows the practice, but only if it is done as part of a general personnel policy. The need for skilled workers throughout the Canadian economy will probably curtail the practice of compulsory retirement further over time.

There remain professions, such as piloting commercial aircraft, in which retirement tends to be a backdoor practice via rigorous medical tests. In such jobs, public safety trumps individual preferences. But airline pilots who build up substantial wealth through their generous paycheques and pension plans have the means to do other work. Those who are active, sharp, and socially adept need not be cowed into retirement any more.

Can't afford to retire. Except for rare cases in which a pension or pensions produce income in excess of what the job pays, there is a definite cost to quitting work permanently. Numerous surveys show that folks approaching retirement have insufficient savings. Although most of these surveys are done by insurance companies and mutual fund vendors that are eager to sell their retirement plans and products, even back-of-the-envelope calculations tend to validate them.

By estimating what financial planners call the Income Replacement Ratio, or IRR, which we discuss in detail in the next chapter, you can see how much retirement income as a fraction of pre-retirement income is needed to maintain a way of life. The IRR adjusts income earned before retirement with expenses after retirement. It is often said to be 70 percent. That means you can maintain your way of life with 70 percent of pre-retirement income when you are retired. The 70 percent figure varies with personal circumstance, but it is a benchmark for retirement planning.

Concern about risk. There is no certainty in life, and even the quip about death and taxes is not quite right. Taxes may be certain, but the tax rate one pays is not. Death is certain, but the timing is unpredictable. For those who have not financed their retirements well with ample capital and pension, annuities, or other sources of income, a long life can be a great burden.

The more money you have, the less the financial risk you have to carry. Financial planners like to assume a constant rate of income or reduction of capital over time, but that ignores the odds that medical science will add years to our ages and life expectancy. Early or premature retirement increases the risk of running out of money.

Risks can manifest themselves in many ways. A company pension plan may not be able to maintain anticipated benefits. You might suffer an uninsured loss, perhaps a major theft or a fire for which insurance compensation is not adequate. A child or grandchild can have financial difficulties that the grandparent wants to help solve.

Risks grow over time if only because the longer the period, the more things there are that can happen. The antidotes to financial risk are insurance for foreseeable loss, diversification of investments, and, of course, having a relatively large rainy-day fund or capital base. The longer you work, the more money you have—it's as simple as that. The implications for unnecessary retirement are obvious. The antidote is as clear. In the end, the decision to stop making money is fraught with peril. It may be wise, but the choice has to be made in light of its consequences.

Exercise: From your personal experience and expectations, argue against retirement. See the summary at the end of this chapter and apply the reasons not to retire to your own situation.

Reasons to Retire

You can afford to quit work. If you have kept working at a job for decades because it would be too costly to give up seniority or supplemental health benefits, then hitting the road when you have enough capital for retirement makes sense. The irony is that many jobs have fringe benefits too rich to abandon. The decision to retire requires that the value of staying on the job be weighed against the income that can be had by quitting work.

Defined benefits pension plans that pay a stipulated amount of money for the life of the former employee, often with indexation to match the cost of living, can be immensely valuable. The concept is to capitalize the flow of money and the money value of benefits and figure out what sum of money would generate those benefits. This is actuarial work, for you are not likely to take all benefits, to have all illnesses covered, and so on. The bottom line is that if continuing to work will boost your pension, it can be too costly to leave. It is no wonder that in human rights legislation, the federal government has left itself the right to terminate employees as a matter of course at defined ages. Otherwise, many would never leave.

You have to go. Compulsory retirement is largely a thing of the past, but in some occupations such as airline pilot and others related to public safety—that's cops and firefighters, locomotive engineers and bus drivers—leaving the job at 60 or 65 has been the norm. The unions representing employees in these groups have challenged the rules, using the broad statutes applicable to all work to justify an end to mandatory retirement in specific jobs. At Air Canada, at the time of writing, pilots are seeking an end to being forced to quit work. There are marketing issues at play, wage issues for senior pilots, and public safety concerns. It is difficult to predict the outcome of the case, but it is a sure thing that airlines and other employers who have to sell services to the public will impose more medical tests and create other barriers to continuing employment of older pilots. Accepting the inevitable, retirement has to be seen as necessary one day.

You want to be near friends and family. In a society built on mobility, the value of being able to have an enduring home is immense. Roots are intangible but precious. So the intended retiree who says, "I want to be with my children while I am still young enough to enjoy them without being a burden to them," makes sense.

It is possible to estimate some of the value of being close to children or golf courses or anything else. If you have spent X dollars per year on flights or other sorts of trips to see the kids, add it up. If it is $10,000 a year, multiply the sum by what you think your remaining life expectancy is. Add on what the kids have spent going to see you. The sum of all of this may be quite large. Compare that sum to the difference between your after-tax income from work and your estimated after-tax retirement income. If you gain more by saving on travel than you give up by quitting work, it is rational to retire. Of course, children grow up and go their own way, have their own children, and move on. Every case is different, but the cost estimation method is the same for every situation.

You have the opportunity and desire to take a buyout. For a variety of reasons, employers apply a combination of carrot-and-stick techniques to remove senior employees taking up space they think might be better occupied by younger employees. As well, organizations that have to downsize to save wage costs may decide that it is better to provide generous incentives to employees to leave.

The incentives may take the form of accelerated pension benefits or cash payments. A pension plan may be structured to reduce or eliminate the benefits of staying on the job for another 5 or 10 years. The employee at age 55 with a bridge to CPP/QPP benefits at age 65, the exhausted time server who just wants to leave, and those who have good jobs or pleasant activities waiting for them may take the buyouts.

They should do it with care, though, for retirement is just that, regardless of the reasons for doing it. However, the problem in assessing a buyout is not so much in evaluating present tradeoffs, but in measuring what the decision may look like in 5 or 10 years. Pencil work is essential, but so is introspection. If the deal is good, sharpen that pencil. If it seems just too good to be true, get advice. And if it really is the promised retirement, then maybe you should take it.

Your pension and savings are so big that you might as well retire. It is not common, but there are people who have put away $2 million in retirement savings, who have qualified for the $10,615 maximum CPP/QPP pension (2008 levels), and who figure that they can get by very nicely on their assets. This level of wealth is possible for senior civil servants married to other senior civil servants, corporate CEOs, successful investment bankers, thrifty dentists and medical specialists who have been careful to manage their practices to maximize retained earnings.

You want to reduce stress. If you hate quarrelsome customers, bullies in the office, endless committee meetings, wretched food in the company cafeteria, the guy in the next cubicle who chomps on raw garlic, or the two-hour commute each way, then go. It is as simple as that.

You want to use retirement assets already in place. You have bought your maisonette in Paris, the island in the Caribbean, or a horse farm in the Eastern Townships, and you want to use it before you die. You can either work out the annual value of the investment or just pack and leave. Either is a rational plan.

> **Exercise:** Think of retirement as liberation and try to look ahead five years. Do you think you will be happy you made the decision to retire? What will retirement have accomplished? What will you have gained, what will you have lost?

10 Reasons Not to Retire

1. No reason to get up in morning
2. Loss of identity
3. Relinquishing perks of employment
4. Loss of company benefits: company car, discount travel, etc.
5. Loss of camaraderie
6. No legal compulsion to retire
7. Inability to live very well on earned income
8. Insufficient savings and investments
9. Apprehension about finances—stock market could tumble
10. Fear of making a one-time, non-recoverable decision

10 Reasons to Retire

1. Desire for freedom, end to 9-to-5 drudgery, lack of respect in office or shop, etc.
2. Health concerns
3. Compulsory retirement for cops, pilots, etc.
4. Desire to move to be near children, friends, Paris, etc. Wish to travel extensively
5. Wish to take a buyout

6. Lack of pension incentive to continue work
7. Lower-stress life
8. Juicy pension benefits
9. Another job waiting, e.g., teaching what you have been doing
10. Rational wish to use an investment, such as a vacation home, already paid for

Chapter 4

Budgeting for the Future

Financial planning is as much an exercise in imagination as it is pencil work. Everyone is inclined to extrapolate from the present to the future, but life does not really work that way. Retirement may be a continuation of a way of life or it may mean living a different life altogether. The trick for constructing a budget is to plan for retirement in stages. After all, what you do from 50 to 60 or 60 to 70 may differ from what you can do in the later stages of your life. So imagining the way your life will change is part of the planning.

You already know from your own life so far that expenses vary with your age. Those who retire in middle age may actually increase their spending during retirement. Moreover, these early retirees may be bypassing the years of their lives when they could earn the most and accumulate the greatest amount of wealth. These are, after all, the years when mortgages are finally paid off, the kids have finished their university education, and when, finally, it is possible to save for retirement. And they are often the years of peak earnings. Those who wait to retire until illness forces it upon them may wind up spending very little. They may be unable to travel very much, have no need for a car, and may have no reason to maintain an elaborate wardrobe. How then can we plan for our retirement when we aren't sure what awaits us? Let's start with what we know.

The simplest way to think of the costs of living is to say that they rise from childhood through school, buying a home, raising children, and saving for retirement. Costs begin to decline as we move to smaller houses or apartments, perhaps capturing capital gains that grew as house prices rose. Food bills may diminish for, as we grow older, we tend to eat less—but food costs are currently on the rise. Clothing costs will represent less of our overall budget. But some costs may go up. Seniors are often more sensitive to cold than younger people. They may keep their houses warmer—no small cost in Canadian winters, especially with the high cost of energy. As a senior, you may have higher uninsured medical and dental expenses. You may need to hire help to maintain your home.

In the end, there are no correct or standard sets of retirement costs. At the time of writing, the U.S. and Canadian dollars are close to parity. In the following table, Consumer Price Index data are used to estimate relative amounts of household spending by category.[1]

In this chapter we'll generate a list of possible expenses that will help to answer the question of how much money will be required to maintain a certain way of life after retirement. This is half the answer to "When can I retire?" The other half, of course, is how much money will be available for retirement. You should obviously aim to have expenses be within income, though if you elect to erode capital as life goes on, then you can spend more freely. However, it is wise to be modest even if you want to die broke, for running out of money before your time is up is a ticket to dependence on others and even to tragedy.

Table 4.1 Average Annual Household Expenditures as a Fraction of
Disposable Income

Category	% of Total Household Expense
Shelter (mortgage or rent)	30
Car ownership	20
Food	15
Pension contributions	10
Utilities	7
Health care	4
Entertainment	4
Clothing	4
Household furnishing	4
Education	2

A Balance of Components

For most people, retirement will involve a reduction of income.
But that reduction will be compensated by lower income taxes; an
end to contributions to the Canada or Quebec Pension Plans;
elimination of Employment Insurance payments, union or professional dues, pension or RRSP contributions, commuting costs, and
perhaps clothes for the office and bar bills for drinks after work.

The measure of the ratio of the income one needs before retirement to the income one needs after retirement is called the Income
Replacement Ratio by financial planners. It is often said to be
70 percent of pre-retirement income, but, in fact, it varies with
individual circumstances. It may be 40 percent and it could be
80 percent. It is a question of style of retirement and of the structure

of income before and after retirement. And that is why it is important to try to estimate it as a part of retirement planning. After all, 50 percent of pre-retirement income is easier to achieve than, say, 80 percent.

By the time you retire, you have probably put your kids through school and have paid off your mortgage and most debts. In retirement, you will no longer contribute to the Canada or Quebec Pension Plans and other retirement funds. Let's say you have been spending $60,000 a year before retirement on day-to-day living, vacations, gifts, and so forth. To see what kind of retirement income you need to support this lifestyle, just add up the expenses you will not have in retirement such as CPP/QPP premiums, mortgage payments if applicable, tuition and related costs, and so on. Take that off the $60,000. Now you have the bare-bones cost of living in retirement. Add on the cost of your hobbies or travel, and you have an adjusted estimate of the annual cost of retirement.

In an analysis of income replacement, authors Bruce Cohen and Brian FitzGerald observe that spending habits of retirees vary inversely with retirement income. In other words, the more money you have for retirement, the lower the fraction of it you are likely to spend. They note a Statistics Canada survey published in 1998 that illustrates the point. Those with pre-retirement incomes of $20,000 to $29,999 needed 62 percent of those incomes for life after retirement. But those earning $70,000 a year or more needed just 45 percent of their pre-retirement incomes to get by.[2]

There are two reasons for the decline in the ratio of expenses to total income. First, many expenses are constant regardless of income. A litre of milk or a box of cornflakes costs the same to the upper-income shoppers as it does to the shopper with a low income. Second, upper-income retirees may accrue wealth in their investments that they leave to compound in stocks, mutual funds, or bank accounts. The money is there to be spent, but since there is no need to draw it, it's left to grow. A Canadian industrialist put it well when he said, "For an average person, turning $10,000 of savings into $20,000 is miraculous. For a wealthy person, turning $10 million into $20 million is merely inevitable."

Anyone can get richer, but it is a lot easier when you are very rich to start with. The wealthy can diversify their assets more easily than the not-quite-rich and those who just get by. Diversification lowers their risk in any one investment—say a single stock or bond or mutual fund—and increases their chances of their fortunes growing larger. The wealthy can afford to take their time with investment returns. Leaving money in an investment tends to increase the odds of having reliable and healthy returns. The affluent can afford better advice or may be able to pay less for it as a fraction of assets under management. Finally, the wealthy may have income taxable in their hands from capital that is intended to be bequeathed to charities or to children. Wealth has its privileges, one of which is that, once achieved, it is easier to keep than to spend. The fact is that the propensity to consume out of income declines as the amount of income increases.[3]

QUESTION: What is the income replacement ratio and what does it mean?

ANSWER: The ratio is the amount of post-retirement income needed to replace pre-retirement income. The replacement ratio eliminates the costs of retirement savings and other work-related expenses, and allows for lower taxes once one has left the labour force.

Housing

There are no rules to explain the cost of housing, which is a very personal choice. You may begin your retirement still living in the large house with eight bathrooms and a vast kitchen that for decades was right for your family of six children. Do you keep the house as a place for visiting children and grandchildren, sell it and move to smaller quarters, or keep the house and renovate it to include one or more apartments that can be rented out for income to pay upkeep and other bills? There are no easy answers, but one thing is certain: You must live someplace. There are alternatives such as living with children, relatives, or friends, or perhaps in an institution, but most folks prefer the independence that goes with a home of one's own. Moreover, that home is likely to have value not just as a capital asset, but also as a foundation of life. Homes have memories, they are roots in the community, and they are anchors for life.

Let's work through an example of housing costs relative to income. Assume that a couple entering retirement has $50,000 a year pre-tax income from a combination of public pension income, company pensions, and Registered Retirement Income Fund payouts. Assume that their house, with a market value of $500,000, is paid for. Annual taxes and estimated maintenance costs are $10,000 a year. Our couple will have $40,000 in after-tax income. Paying a quarter of that income just in property taxes and maintenance expenses is far too much. Add in the opportunity cost of owning property rather than having some of the $500,000 in a high-interest bank account, bonds, or a diversified mix of stocks with secure dividends and you can see that the occupants of this house are actually house poor. The upside of the high cost of this accommodation is that the price of the house may rise over time.

If the house price rises 10 percent or $50,000 per year, then the real estate market will, in a sense, be paying for the occupants' cost of living.

The question then becomes one of balancing current expenses with future wealth. If the house is a principal residence, then any capital gains realized at sale will be immune from tax. But at some point, the owners have to decide if they will cash in their investment or retain the property for their heirs.

If the $500,000 house has appreciated to, say, $2 million, which it would in about 15 years, assuming that the house market pushes up prices by 10 percent per year, and if consumer prices have substantially lagged house price gains, the owners might want to cash in. If the appreciation is higher, say to $5 million, it is even more likely that they will want to increase their choices and do more with their lives than remain custodians of an expensive house.

The example illustrates the problem of asset ownership. A house provides both value in use and potential value in investment. When the investment or market value of the house is above the value of the house as shelter, it may be helpful to evaluate sale. In the opposite case, a house that is valuable in use but has little investment value— for example, a nice house in a town in which the one industry, perhaps a mine, has shut down—the investment value may be very low. If the house cannot even fetch a bid, the occupants may have no choice but to stay. Without the house, they would be in the position of having to start over with their financial lives.

There is a comparable situation in the case of a house or condo that is declining in investment value. If the decline is irreversible, as it would be in the case of adverse neighbourhood change, then occupancy costs should be increased to include the loss of resale value. In other words, if the house is in a state of decay or if neighbourhood house prices are tumbling, then the owners should figure in what amounts to a depreciation charge every year and save up a fund that will help them buy another house. The cost of moving, if that is the choice, will be a budget item and should be part of retirement costs. In sum, if you have to move, save up for it.

Estimating home ownership costs is one of the most difficult financial planning problems. Unlike setting a budget for clothing, which is easily adjustable to reduce monthly costs, or for travel, for which one can just forego a trip once in a while, the house budget is lumpy. There may be unexpected expenses for a new furnace, for example. Downsizing to a smaller house has substantial transaction costs: lawyers, real estate commissions, moving vans, breakage, and emotional turmoil. Weighing staying in your existing home against buying a smaller one, which may be full of unknown problems, is never easy. But there are some golden rules you should start to follow in mid-life: Don't defer routine or major maintenance until your income has declined to retirement levels, definitely get the mortgage paid off before retirement begins, and in retirement don't buy more house than you need.

The homeowner with too much house in retirement may have a problem—in effect, it's a forced marriage to a large chunk of wealth stuck in a property. The homeowner who has a modest house in retirement will have the flexibility to improve the house or perhaps to buy a second home. In housing expense planning, modesty pays.

Food

Everybody has to eat, but the range of costs to satisfy that need is immense. The older you get, the fewer calories you need and the less you tend to eat. Add to that the fact that the free time you have in retirement can be spent shopping carefully and preparing more meals from scratch, and the possibilities for cost control grow. After all, when free time is abundant, there is no need to pay a premium for prepared foods or restaurant meals.

Setting a budget for food is a relatively easy matter of keeping track of pre-retirement food spending and adjusting the budget for age and free time. If you have spent $600 a month for food for two before retirement, $600 a month will work in retirement too. Assuming no change in the food budget amounts to charging inflation to the pre-retirement cost of food. That, in turn, means eating less or at least spending less. So estimating that food prices will rise over time is reasonable. Allow perhaps 3 percent per year and work forward for a decade or two. In 10 years, food prices will be up 34 percent, in 20 years, they will be up 81 percent.

The opportunities for reducing the amount you spend on food and increasing the nutrition value are great. Here's an example: The food processing industry is highly specialized and hugely profitable. Packaged breakfast cereals made with a bit of corn or wheat and large amounts of corn syrup, fructose, sucrose, etc., are candy with some crunch. The stuff is ridiculously expensive, contains advertising as a principal ingredient, and is usually compounded and packaged to appeal to children. If you want cereal, make your own granola or oatmeal. It is quick to do, will save you a fortune, and is better for you. The cost of some boxed muesli cereals works out to 75 cents to a dollar a serving. You can make it yourself for a nickel a serving. Do the math: 70 cents per year for, say, 250 days a year—this allows for variety in munching—is a saving of $175.00! Likewise, the synthetic cheeses sold by major food processors, salty snacks, microwave popcorn, and high-fat salad dressings can either be replicated at home with raw ingredients or, in the case of the transfat-loaded, sugar- and salt-laden products, skipped in the interests of health. There is evidence that links junk foods to serotonin issues in depression.[4] Buy raw, fresh foods and you will save money and be healthier. Here endeth this lecture.

Transportation

Transportation—whether you drive a Bentley or take the bus—is a variable and highly controllable expense. The annual costs of car ownership, which include gas, oil, repairs, and, of course, depreciation, tend to be quite large. On the other hand, in many areas, there is no substitute for a car or small truck. Canada is huge and public transport serves only a tiny fraction of the national geography.

The costs of ownership of even average cars is surprisingly high. For example, ownership and use of a 2007 Honda Accord four-door sedan "Special Edition" costs US$10,727 per year for five years. Depreciation is the largest expense in the first year. Financing costs of $4,028 are a large cost, as is estimated fuel of $8,231.[5] Some may object that a Honda Accord is not quite an economy car, but the cost range for medium compacts varies from $27,850 for a Chevy Cobalt LT to $34,765 for a Ford Taurus SE over five years.[6]

In retirement, these high costs can be reduced by several steps. First, keep cars in good running order. Surveys show that cars kept until they are 15 years old minimize ownership costs. You can choose to buy good used cars and save high depreciation charges. Pay cash and avoid finance and leasing charges. However, when manufacturers offer interest-free or very low interest finance charges, it pays to investigate the deals.

Sometimes people enter retirement with a small fleet of vehicles. If a couple has kept two cars and paid the depreciation, maintenance, insurance, repairs, and gas bills for both, there is an obvious economy in downsizing to just one car.

If economy is a concern, you should also stick to cars with relatively low upkeep. Prestigious foreign brands are infamous for the astonishing cost of parts aggravated by the monopolies manufacturers give to dealers in many cities. Compare the cost of fixing common problems on high-profile foreign cars with the cost of fixing the same problems on domestic makes. Fancy foreign makes often have no independent secondary parts suppliers. There is no choice but buying parts from the local dealer. Once you get over the shock of buying replacement parts, you may pick the domestic car. "Porsche. There is no substitute" says it all. A Corvette, however, is a Chevrolet. Prestige and precision have a price. It is good to decide before you retire what a ride is worth. An alternative to ownership is rental when necessity requires.

Travel

There is no category of spending that is as variable and perhaps as unknowable as travel costs. When you have more leisure time, travel is a way to fill it. What's more, discretionary travel is more affordable than business travel. Buy your tour to visit Bulgaria months in advance and you can go for a song. If you have no expected conflicting appointments, you can join the Last Minute Club or a similar plan and get incredible deals for what amounts to filling up empty seats on a plane or hotel rooms a travel company overbought.

Every person handles travel differently. For some, it will be a pricey motor home such as a Triple E Empress Elite, which, depending on the exact model, is priced north of US$300,000 plus options such as a power awning. Plus tax, of course. Not everyone wants to pilot a 34,000-pound, 40-foot-long critter that, when you take away the lovely interior appointments, is a bus. But the luxobarge is a terrific choice for those who would rather not bother with hotels—and have the money to fill it with pricey gas. There are boats and yachts, personal aircraft, weekends in Paris, or, for the economical, canoeing and hiking. As the saying goes, there is no accounting for taste.

When you're drawing up your retirement plans, it is possible to set budget parameters for travel. The following table is a guide to what you can have with various levels of retirement income.

Table 4.2 Travel Planning by Income Level

Net after-tax income range	Potential style of travel	Notional cost/year
$15,000–$30,000	Stay with friends, camp	$1,000–$3,000
$30,000–$50,000	Discount travel, budget deals	$3,000–$8,000
$50,000–$80,000	Cruises, good hotels	$8,000–$20,000
$80,000–$150,000	Fine spas, business class airfare	$20,000–$40,000
$150,000–$300,000	Best hotels, first-class airfare	$40,000–$80,000
$300,000 and up	Villas and yachts	$80,000–

Rather than try to predict what you can or should spend on travel, it is best to leave it as a residual budget category. In other words, figure out the cost of everything else and then see what is left for travel.

Health Care

Residents of Canada have their basic health care costs covered. Those who spend more than 180 days of any year living outside of

Canada may not have their coverage maintained by provincial plans. But for those covered, the implicit costs of medical care tend to rise with age. Canada's system of provincial health care plans takes care of costs for those who live here. The high potential medical and hospital cost of being over 60 or 65 becomes apparent when you have to buy travel health coverage. Costly it may be, but it is also essential. If you plan to be away from Canada for substantial periods, check costs in your province and put them into your retirement budget.

I am not suggesting you load up on supplemental health insurance. Insurance plans that cover entirely routine procedures such as annual or semi-annual dental checkups tend to have little advantage. For each dollar of dental hygiene expense, they charge a dollar of extra premium. The most these plans do is allow easy budgeting and cost averaging. There may be valuable fringe benefits to extended-care plans, however, so each plan should be studied closely.

The cost range of various plans is too large for inclusion in *When Can I Retire?* so you should shop around for coverage.[7] For those who can afford it, membership in a private medical plan for fees that range from $2,500 to $10,000 a year can eliminate the long waits for examination and treatment in Canada's public health care system. Former Prime Minister Paul Martin, a champion of public health care, is known to have used private health care. Though Canadians may support or criticize the public health care system, when serious illness arises and speed counts, those who can afford it head for the United States. And for discretionary surgery, increasing numbers go to Thailand and India for quality care at very low prices.[8]

Drug Expenses

Coverage of drug expenses by provincial insurance plans varies across Canada. There is no consistency in cost, deductibles, co-payment requirements by the insured, or annual maximums that beneficiaries have to pay.

All provinces do not charge premiums to people with low incomes. Deductibles vary from nothing for everyone in Alberta, Nova Scotia, New Brunswick, Prince Edward Island, and Newfoundland and Labrador to Manitoba's complex formula that pays only sums greater than 5.51 percent of adjusted net annual household income for people with adjusted net annual household incomes over $75,000. Co-payment varies from 35 percent of prescription cost in Saskatchewan to zero in Manitoba, subject to the complex Manitoba deductibility rules. For those who receive the Guaranteed Income Supplement, Quebec is the most generous province with no deductible, no co-payment, and no maximum annual beneficiary contribution.[9] An excellent summary of costs and benefits of drug plans can be found in the February 12, 2008, issue of the Canadian Medical Association Journal, accessible online at http://www.cmaj.ca/cgi/content/full/178/4/405.

Personal Expenses

There is a vast range of personal items in most folks' monthly budgets—grooming, cosmetics, spa treatments, visits to herbalists, acupuncture, and much more. A great deal of this spending is not even included in budgets, for people tend to regard many of these items as being too small to track. Collectively, when they add up to a few hundred dollars a month, they are not small. Add in clothing for a few hundred dollars more per month and coffee at Starbucks or the like—at what could be $5 a day or 20 working days per month that works out to $100, and when you include weekend forays for coffee and whipped cream concoctions, the tab grows larger.

Some books masquerading as financial planning guides suggest that one can forego the cappuccino and grow wealthy by saving and investing coffee money. Multiply $5 a day for a fancy coffee by five days per week for 50 working weeks a year and you get $1,250 you can bank each year. The skip-the-coffee theory of building capital is not wrong. The economic issue, however, is to find a balance between the pleasure of coffee and snacks and the future value of what the money will earn. It's a personal thing. Review what you spend on coffee and snacks, gum and candy bars, and other diet wreckers and what you spend on personal decoration, and ask if the money could be used to better effect elsewhere. Chances are, it can, but penny-pinching is not likely to be the way to build much capital. I might add that sweetened coffee that amounts to liquefied candy harms the body as well as the wallet, but then I'd be preaching again.

Charity, Gifts, and Bequests

We tend to think of charitable giving as a residual category. In this sense, we give what we can after other needs are covered. But there are other concepts of charitable giving. One is tithing, which raises the priority of giving from residue to high duty. Some people have agreed to fund a charity or project over a period of one year. Finally, there are some people who have established family trusts or Registered Education Savings Plans for children or grandchildren and who feel obliged to keep the money flowing into them.

Good works are a personal value. This book can make no judgment of their worth. At the same time, if you are inclined toward giving, it is a good idea to get tax deductions for those good works. If you are not sure of the standing of a charity, you can check it at the Canada Revenue Agency website. Visit http://www.cra-arc.gc.ca/tx/chrts/dnrs/menu-eng.html, where you'll find extensive information on what an organization does and the state of its finances, and you can verify that it can provide tax receipts for contributions. Charitable qualification status and financial information can be found for U.S. charities at http://www.irs.gov/charities/index.html.

When it comes to giving to children and grandchildren, friends, the mailman at Christmas, and gifts for friends, the issues are not merely financial. Gifts of money for post-secondary education for children or grandchildren produce no tax deductions, save for transferable unused student credits, but when put into Registered Education Savings Plans have no tax on investment gains. When assets are distributed to beneficiaries, they have to pay tax, but usually at the low or even zero rates for which students qualify.

Gifts and donations involve philosophical principles. We give to show we care. We give because it is expected. We give because the psychological cost of not tipping the waiter or the cab driver is higher than we care to bear. The economic efficiency of giving just to be nice is questionable, though one can rationalize it. But it is a fact that most of us do make gifts to others that are expenditures no different than any other personal items. At the same time, the customs of giving can be made both more efficient and more satisfying. Try ranking your charitable priorities and comparing them to amounts given. You may wind up giving less and feeling better. Or giving more and feeling fine. The value is in the exercise.

The Stages of Retirement

It makes sense to break retirement down into stages of early and late retirement. The first stage of retirement takes in the years from 65 to 75. After that, Stage 2 kicks in. As life spans increase, these rather arbitrary stages may change and, like any attempt to put people into categories, there are many people who stay in Stage 1 even when they are in their eighties. Let's consider some principles:

- Retirees are cautious spenders. Fear of running out of money trumps the fact that it may cost less to live in retirement than in the time before retirement.
- The ability to spend may grow over time if you continue to save and invest.
- The need to consume declines with age and the shrinkage of households through the death of a partner.
- Wealth may rise over time through appreciation.
- With declining consumption, the cost of living as measured by conventional Consumer Price Index numbers will tend to fall. If measured by a tailored index that eliminates such things as mortgage costs and diapers, it may decline even more.
- Retirees can control their spending quite well.
- Public assistance programs such as subsidized transportation can reduce costs.

We can set up a spending program that adjusts for age and stage of retirement. In the following table we assume the annual household budget is $50,000.

Remember, the numbers and categories used in Table 4.3 are merely examples. Your percentages or actual dollars will vary, as will the categories that are important to you. In this example, saving capacity rises over time because the retiree(s) have less capacity to do things as they get older. A chart that shows expenses rising with levels of care needed could also be prepared.

Table 4.3 Standardized Spending by Stage of Retirement

Category	Stage 1: 65 to 75		Stage 2: 75 and up	
	% of Total Expense	$	% of Total Expense	$
Shelter (mortgage or rent)	30	$15,000	30	$15,000
Car ownership or transportation	16	8,000	10	5,000[1]
Food	11	5,500	10	5,000
Pension contributions	0	0	0	0
Utilities	7	3,500	7	3,500
Health care	6	3,000	10	5,000[2]
Entertainment	5	2,500	2	1,000
Clothing	4	2,000	2	1,000
Household furnishing	4	2,000	2	1,000
Education and reading	2	1,000	2	1,000
Travel	10	5,000	2	1,000
Personal care	2	1,000	20	10,000[3]
Saving	3	1,500	3	1,500

Notes to table:
[1] *It is assumed that in later life, the retired person uses taxis and bus transportation.*
[2] *With increasing age goes added reliance on drugs and assistance that may not be insured services.*
[3] *In old age, one tends to rely on home care services that may not be insured.*

To build your own expense table, begin with the life you have lived up to retirement. Consider the nature of your expenses. If you rent, then shelter is a flow of cash. If you are paying down a mortgage, shelter expenses are a cash expense with a compensating gain of personal wealth on your balance sheet. If your mortgage is

paid off in full, then shelter is just a matter of repair and maintenance, though the money that is tied up in the house or condo is
still an expense in the sense of an opportunity cost—that is, money
that could be used elsewhere.

If you live in a city or town, you can use public transport and
taxis more easily than if you live in a rural area. For travel, it is
often the case that older people find it harder to get around than
when they were younger. Still, if you have a home in Florida and
children in Canada, travel expenses may remain high or even rise if
you subsidize trips by grandchildren from Canada. Saving is the
residue of income that is not spent. In our table, saving rises with
age. But if you make charitable donations, it is possible that giving
would also rise with age. Each person is different. To that end, the
following worksheet expands the standard categories and allows
you to build a personalized spending model. Adjust for inflation by
adding, say, 2.5 percent per year, a rate that is a current consensus
of economists and investment dealers for expected inflation for the
next few decades. You can estimate at 3 percent per year for a
margin of safety.

Table 4.4 Individualized Spending by Stage of Retirement

	Stage 1: 65 to 75		Stage 2: 75 and up	
Category	% of Total Expense	$	% of Total Expense	$
Shelter (mortgage or rent)				
Car ownership or transportation				
Food				
Utilities				
Health care				

Table 4.4 Continued

Entertainment
Clothing
Household furnishing
Education and reading
Travel and vacations
Personal care
Grooming
Donations and gifts
Saving
TOTAL

Controlling Expenses in Retirement

Traditionally, the elderly were poor. Today, the elderly are often rather well off. In statistical terms, those over age 45 are net creditors of the financial system, for they have paid off most of their debts and have positive net worth.

Some people approaching retirement age may be worried when they read reports published by advocacy groups like the Canadian Council for Social Development, which promotes the idea that the elderly, whose incomes may be below a given cutoff line, are poor. But the cutoff line is arbitrary. A cutoff line that says a family with a gross income less than 40 percent of the national average is poor is misleading. After all, if everyone's real income rose by 100 percent, then the below-40-percent group would still be "poor" by the abstract yardstick. Moreover, the standard measure of one yardstick for all fails to distinguish the expenses of the elderly. As we have seen, those who are retired tend to have expenses different from those of people who are still working.

Beware of being misled by percentage cutoff lines: They are arbitrary. They don't reflect the ability of some people to make their own clothes or do their own car repairs, the preferences of some to refrain from alcohol and others to have a fine scotch before dinner, etc. Your expenses are a statement of who you are. It is possible to live well on $30,000 a year and to live badly on $100,000 a year.

Rather than dwell on a procedure for defining income levels, we can accept that budgets are relative, but add the qualification that the elderly have the ability to control their spending more than active workers, who have to cope with employment costs.

The problem of spending is therefore relative to need and the expected length of retirement. If in retirement you find that your expenses are greater than you had foreseen, the obvious course is to reduce spending in areas such as entertainment, a field that can include books, movies, plays, sports, etc.; travel; grooming; and, of course, charitable giving.

With more time to spend, you may find it difficult to fill the gap left by cutbacks in entertainment and travel. Rather than do less of either, try thinking of it as spending less money but getting more value for each dollar. That can often be done by more careful shopping for entertainment and travel. With more time, you can take the best deals, go for matinees rather than evening performances, turn a meal into a recreation—as in fishing for one's dinner—and use libraries rather than bookstores. The hunt becomes its own financial reward.

That reward is hard to see, however, if you pay the full price when you buy things or pay for them over time with credit cards, bank lines of credit, or other forms of borrowing. Not only does paying by instalment raise the total price paid enormously, but it makes tracking expenses more difficult.

QUESTION: What are some of the ways to cut spending in retirement?

ANSWER: Focus on variable costs such as food—use fewer prepared foods and cook from scratch; transportation—keep cars longer and make more use of public transport; travel— fly when prices are lowest, consider joining organizations that fill up unused seats on charters; clothing—shop harder and worry less about fashion trends; incidentals—be vigilant.

Saving

It may seem a contradiction, but it is important to save in retirement for, yes, retirement. The reason is simple: Things happen beyond what you have planned. For example, a child, grown and with a life of his or her own, may encounter difficulties and want to move back in with mum and dad. You may find yourself looking after the grown child's own children. You may have unexpected but substantial medical bills to pay, high repair costs for a house foundation, or the need to replace a car ahead of what may have been anticipated. The cost of home heating, gas for the car, and food are all dependent on the price of oil, which has been volatile and is predicted to continue climbing.

Having a cash reserve can make the difference between living as one planned and having to borrow to pay unexpected bills and meet rising energy costs. So the question arises: How much should you save?

Cash flow alone does not give the answer, for a person with $100,000 a year in retirement income may have more obligations than someone with just $20,000 a year of income. The point is that you have to plan not just to meet expenses, but to have enough income in retirement to allow for a surplus.

How much to allow for an emergency fund is not a fixed amount. For those who are employed, a rule of thumb is to have a fund with three months' income for emergencies. That rule can be carried forward into retirement. Once the fund is built, it can be maintained with only a small contribution each month to cover inflation and perhaps to build up additional financial protection.

Review and Sensitivity

You may be disappointed that, so far, I have not set down any hard and fast guidelines for retirement budgets. That can be defended as intellectual honesty, for no one can tell another person how to live and no person can predict his or her life's condition many decades in the future. What I can suggest as an alternative to rigid budgets is periodic review. At least once a year, go over your expenses and compare them to your needs. The review process should examine not only current spending and income, but attempt to weigh present needs with future needs, just as you did when you were drawing up your first retirement budget.

Good plans have to be changeable. The Scots poet Robert Burns (1759–1796) wrote, "The best laid schemes o' mice an' men gang aft a-gley," which, with the burrs removed, means "the plans of mice and men often go wrong." Translated into financial planning terms and attached to assets, Burns's comment implies that you should prepare for several outcomes. In making spending plans, such as gifts to children, you can designate the recipient but retain the cash or other assets until a later date. You have the goodwill and presumably the gratitude, but you also keep the cash under your control. Of course, if the recipient needs the money soon or if there are good tax reasons to hasten a bequest, then take suitable advice and act accordingly.

The sensitivity component of a review is the subtext to dollars and cents calculations. Giving up driving implies a loss of mobility and control over one's life. And that may be true even if you replace the Benz with a car service. Giving up a grand old house for a condo that is really just a box among many boxes can imply a loss of identity or a severing of roots. Rather than sell an asset like a house, consider the middle ground: renting out a portion of the house or making an arrangement that the tenant pay some or all of the rent in personal services. If getting up and down the stairs is problematic, consider buying a stair lift. However, you may surprise yourself and be glad to be free of the responsibility for the upkeep of a house. Moving to a condo or retirement home can be life-affirming, rather than a sad alternative.

Table 4.5 Cost Trends in Retirement

Food	It is likely to grow more expensive as fuel costs rise and push up farm and transportation costs.
Travel	Basic costs may rise with the cost of fuel, but highly competitive discount airfares, especially in Europe, may keep them reasonable.
Shelter	If you are keeping your house, don't worry unless you have deferred a great deal of maintenance. If you want to buy a home in a retirement community, try to avoid buying in a frenzy of enthusiasm. After all, Miami condos that rose in price by 100 percent per year a few years ago became dregs on the market with foreclosures having slashed prices by half or more in many south Florida communities.
Clubs	There are no rules. If your gym has always had a senior discount, you can assume it will continue

Utilities	They will go up, for utilities tend to be retail monopolies and are closely related to the cost of producing energy.
Clothing	If you don't need a rack of suits for the office, dressing should be cheaper.
Hobbies, charities, gifts	These categories are always discretionary.
Debt service charges	Retirement is better without a mantle of debt, but whether interest rates will be up or down in 2015 compared to today is beyond prediction.

Chapter 5

Where Will the Money Come From? Public Pensions

For most Canadians, public pensions are the foundation of their retirement. The Canada and Quebec Pension Plans as well as Old Age Security and the Guaranteed Income Supplement will provide at least a minimum standard of living. Each of these plans is indexed to changes in the cost of living. For those dependent on private savings without indexation or other guaranteed ways of pacing inflation, the indexation is vital. Moreover, the longer you live and the more inflation depreciates the dollar, the more critical indexation becomes in the process of matching incomes to rising prices.

In this chapter we'll review the sources of retirement income to which one has become entitled through age and work: Regulations are frequently changed in this area of law and administration, so you should check with Service Canada, the Canada Revenue Agency, and/or your own tax professional or financial advisor to determine the status of rules applicable to your situation. This chapter covers the Canada and Quebec Pension Plans, Old Age Security, and the Guaranteed Income Supplement and discusses management of the clawback provisions that reduce or eliminate the benefits of OAS for people with middle- and upper-level incomes. Worksheets for estimating public pensions as well as employment-based and private pensions discussed in the next chapter can be found in an appendix at the end of Chapter 6. Canada Pension Plan and Quebec Pension Plan benefits are identical for many categories of benefits. The age 65 retirement benefits are the same, for example, though benefits for children of disabled or deceased contributors vary between the plans. It is wise to check with the programs when benefit issues arise.

When I Googled the phrase "retirement income calculator," the internet came up with 631,000 hits. The Government of Canada, several insurance companies, and many financial planners have chimed in with variations of calculation methods. Needless to say, a computer with a simple Excel spreadsheet can tote up sources of income and manipulate results as you plug in different numbers. You can see what difference a change in interest rates will make, for example.

Each calculator uses a fundamental assumption in its method of assessing retirement income. The assumption relates to the ratio of retirement income to annual career or job income required to maintain a certain level of spending. The ratio differs from program to program, and financial planner to financial planner. For example, a recent retirement income calculator from Fidelity Investments estimates from a survey of 2,200 households that Canadians heading into retirement will be able to replace only half their pre-retirement income. Fidelity believes that 80 percent is the better replacement goal. You can find Fidelity's calculator at http://www.fidelity.ca/takethechallenge. Its virtue is that it is fairly simple to use. The 80 percent figure is at the high end of the conventional range. The distinguished Canadian actuary Malcolm Hamilton suggests you can have a good retirement with just half of your pre-retirement income.

No one ratio or formula fits everyone. Those who enter retirement with heavy debts or those who have lost assets to insolvency or divorce may need more public pension money in retirement. However, as a place to begin, and stressing that the 80 percent replacement ratio is rather high, the Fidelity calculation engine may be useful.[1]

It may be more helpful to see the replacement ratio as a sliding scale on which, depending on age and circumstance, spending in retirement may begin high and decline or, perhaps, begin low and rise. The trend varies with the case.

Starting high and declining would be the pattern of someone retiring in good health and trying to fulfill the travel dreams of a lifetime. After years of cruising or of safaris or what have you, he or she might return home to less exotic and less costly pursuits, then become sedentary, then move into assisted housing.

Starting low and finding expenses rising could be the pattern of someone who begins a modest retirement, becomes ill, and elects to spend remaining assets on uninsured medical treatments in the United States or in European spas.

So can the replacement ratio be assumed or planned? Yes, if the retirement plan involves costly pursuits. And yes if the plan means that no expense will be spared as life winds down. In the end, statistical surveys of average behaviour probably mean little. It is individual intent that counts the most.

The Structure of the Canadian Pension System

There are four levels in Canada's pension system:

1. Public pensions, made up of Old Age Security and the Guaranteed Income Supplement, the Canada Pension Plan, and its partner, the Quebec Pension Plan.
2. Employment-based pensions, made up of defined benefit and defined contribution plans.
3. Individual savings plans, made up of Registered Retirement Savings Plans, Life Income Funds, Locked-in Retirement Accounts, and Locked-in Retirement Income Funds.
4. Insurance-based pensions, made up of pensions funded by ordinary life policies and annuities.

Public Pensions

Old Age Security

Canada's Old Age Security system has its philosophical base in 19th-century Prussia. Otto von Bismarck, the man who amalgamated the Hohenzollern dynasty's holdings into Germany at the eve of the 20th century, co-opted left-wing demands for social services by creating the world's first publicly funded national pension plan in 1889. The age of eligibility was 70 at a time when life expectancy was far less. The idea was picked up in Great Britain and across Europe, spread across to the Dominions, and became part of Canadian social welfare when Parliament passed the first old age pension act in 1927. The plans were inexpensive to operate because most people never got to the age when benefits would begin.

There was quibbling about who would pay—Ottawa or the provinces. The decision, a very Canadian one, was to slice the responsibility in half. A strict means test was in effect until 1951, when the federal government made the system universal and ended the means test. Today, Old Age Security, the successor to the 1927 plan, is supplemented with the means-tested Guaranteed Income Supplement. Moreover, the age-dependent pension system is indexed to the rate of inflation. The system is reasonable and humane. It is not as generous as U.S. Social Security or many European pension systems, but it is also less costly for contributors.

As of fall 2008, the OAS payout was a monthly maximum of $516.96. It is reviewed and adjusted quarterly in January, April, July, and October. OAS eligibility is relatively straightforward. If you are 65 years of age and have lived in Canada for 40 years after age 18, you qualify for full OAS. If you have resided in Canada for at least 10 years prior to eligibility of OAS, you will qualify for partial payment. Those who lived in Canada before July 1, 1977, after reaching age 18 or possessed a valid immigration visa on July 1, 1977, have to delve into the rules for eligibility. Even where not fully eligible, people age 65 or over may be able to get fractional OAS equal to the ratio of the years in Canada over age 18 divided by 40 and all this multiplied by the current maximum payment. For more information, go to http://www.hrsdc.gc.ca/en/isp/oas/oastoc.shtml.

Once full or partial OAS pension payments have been approved, they may be paid indefinitely even if you reside outside of Canada provided that you lived in Canada for at least 20 years after reaching 18 years of age. Otherwise, payment may be made only for the month of your departure from Canada and for six additional months, after which time payments are suspended. The pension flow can be resumed if you return to Canada to live.

Old Age Security was intended in its early days to be a universal pension for the elderly. Some question whether it will be part of Canadian social policy and planning in the future. The program is

QUESTION: What are the main qualifications for receiving Old Age Security?

ANSWER: Attaining age 65 and having lived in Canada for at least 10 of the last 40 years after age 18.

immensely expensive, so several governments have tried to impair its universality. The Mulroney government tried to end indexation in 1985 but was defeated by opposition from seniors' groups and a few very articulate individuals who spoke up and made the government of the day fearful of losing seniors' votes. Four years later, the clawback was introduced. It complicates pension planning, for while the issue is simple—Parliament doesn't want to use public funds to pay pensions to people it thinks don't need them—it creates thorny tax issues.

The clawback, a means test retroactively imposed on OAS recipients, begins when an individual's net income exceeds a limit, which is $64,718 in 2008. Over this sum, it takes 15 percent of each additional dollar of net income. The clawback ends with a 100 percent recovery at approximately $105,000 of net income. In other words, if your net income exceeds $105,000, you will lose 100 percent of Old Age Security payments via the clawback.

There are ways to mitigate and even to avoid the clawback. All of them involve income splitting by manipulating the cash flowing into individual net income or by excluding OAS income from Canadian taxation by changing your residence to a different country.

1. Make spousal RRSP contributions to split income that will be paid from RRSPs when you retire. This puts your RRSP

contributions into two hands and reduces the net income of the higher income earner when it comes time to tap the RRSP via a Registered Retirement Income Fund, the most common payout mechanism for RRSPs.

2. Postpone withdrawals from RRSPs until age 71. You get a longer deferral of income tax and you are able to reduce the income base on which the OAS clawback is calculated. An alternative strategy is to begin RRSP withdrawals early in order to average income over a longer period. It is important not to let tax minimization tactics dominate investment plans, however. Clearly, if the returns on your investments are high, say 8 percent per year or more, it is better to keep as much money as possible at work. If returns are below 8 percent, early withdrawal can make more sense.

3. Try to reduce dividends and to increase capital gains. Dividends are increased for tax purposes by 45 percent, which adds to your net income. Although there is a tax credit associated with dividends, it comes later in tax calculations. However, the artificial calculation of dividends used in the Canadian income tax system boosts net income and thereby increases exposure to the clawback. But capital gains in amounts equal to dividends before tax calculation actually reduce net income because only half the gain goes into net income. It follows that stock buybacks by companies are comparatively good because they tend to raise stock prices and add to potential capital gains. Dividend increases are comparatively bad in that they disproportionately raise the taxpayer's income and accelerate the clawback. The bias against dividends in the calculation of the clawback is prejudicial to seniors who ought to be able to count on steady dividend income rather than hit or miss capital gains.

4. Average CPP/QPP by starting benefits at age 60. There is much debate on whether this strategy is optimal in the long run. Life expectancy obviously plays a part. Women, with a longer life expectancy than men, have more reason not to take early CPP benefits. For men, it is wise to take early CPP benefits. If you take CPP/QPP early, you stop contributions, which is good in the sense that you pay less total income tax after CPP/QPP contributions cease, but bad in that you limit your pension base and, if raises are in order, you may wind up penny wise and pound foolish. However, if you expect your income to be constant, then taking early CPP/QPP is a reasonable move. Moreover, the self-employed pay double the individual employee's CPP contribution, that is, they pay their own contribution as well as that of the employer. Thus the self-employed have more incentive to cash in early than those who are employed by other people.

5. If you have or expect substantial investment income, consider transferring the investments to a separate tax entity such as a holding company or a trust. The transfer will crystallize any gains and may accelerate taxation of them. Such a move should be planned with a tax accountant. There are costs to setting up corporations and trusts and the purpose really ought to be more than just tax planning. These structures can insulate assets from some suits for losses and damages. Wealthy individuals use them, but there is no reason that so-called average Canadians should not employ them as well. If the benefits of establishing a corporation or a trust exceed setup costs and annual costs for filing corporate or trust returns, then there is a financially efficient case for going through the exercise.

6. Reduce cash flow that turns into net income by making use of the Tax-Free Savings Account (TFSA) introduced in the

February 2008 federal budget. Beginning in 2009, it allows you to take money on which income tax has been paid, put it into a TFSA, and exempt both the principal and any interest, dividends, or capital gains accrued in the account from federal taxation. Each year, you can put a maximum of $5,000 into a TFSA. If that money produces 6 percent annual return, that would remove $300 from each partner's taxable income each year. For a couple, with two separate TFSAs, the tax-free accruing income would be $600 per year on the same return assumption.

7. If you are moving to the United States or another country, be sure to check tax treaties. You can find a list of countries and a summary of their taxes and how they relate to Canadian pension income at http://www1.servicecanada.gc.ca/en/isp/pub/nontax.shtml. This is a complex question and you should obtain advice from a tax professional before establishing residence in another country.

Guaranteed Income Supplement

The concept of a guaranteed income supplement was rooted in the notion of a negative income tax, an academic idea popular in the 1960s that would use tax returns rather than social workers to get money to the needy. The theory was that just giving money to people whose net income was below a certain line would provide for administrative efficiency and preserve the dignity of the poor. When the Canada Pension Plan and the Quebec Pension Plan went into operation on January 1, 1966, Ottawa recognized that many retirees would not have significant benefits from either plan and that OAS payments would be insufficient to feed, clothe, and house many pensioners. Therefore, the Guaranteed Income Supplement, intended as a bridge to a time when more people would have more income from the CPP/QPP, was introduced. It has become a fixture of the national pension system.

The intent of the GIS program is compassionate. In recognition that OAS is not itself sufficient to provide a living income, the GIS makes up the shortfall for those who fall below a certain income level. As of the second quarter of 2008, the plan was paying up to $652.51 to single people with incomes less than $23.99 per year.

The Guaranteed Income Supplement goes to about a third of all OAS recipients. The main groups of recipients are elderly single women and widows. They are the core of what one might call the embedded poverty of age. Either because of a decision to stay home and raise children, the custom of having a husband as a sole bread-winner, or a history of working casually, even for cash payments and without registration for CPP and QPP benefits, this mostly female core of elderly, impoverished people has not got sufficient income to support themselves in old age. It appears that they will continue to receive the GIS for an indefinite period.

Supplementary Programs

The concept of the GIS actually has three parts. First, two payments are hooked to Old Age Security but technically are not part of it. These are the Spouse's Allowance and the Survivor's Allowance. The GIS is the third component of this triad of benefits.

The Spouse's Allowance, technically called the Allowance, is paid to those who qualify by an income test and who are at least 60 years of age but below age 65, who have been in Canada for 10 years, who were married to a pensioner who was receiving the Guaranteed Income Supplement, and who meet a low income test. The Allowance for the Survivor is for low-income widows and widowers who are 60 to 64 years old. Each benefit is payable to those persons who were in opposite-sex or same-sex relationships for at least 12 months at the time of the death of the spouse or common-law partner. It has a maximum payout for someone with no other income of $1,028.06 per month. The threshold for qualification is income below $20,664 in 2008. This is the income test for someone who is a survivor of a recognized relationship and who is living alone. For the spouse to qualify for the Allowance, the couple's combined income must be below $28,368.

The Allowance stops if the beneficiary is absent from Canada for more than six months, turns 65, or dies. If the couple were separated for more than three months, were divorced, or if the spouse had lost his or her qualification for GIS, the Allowance will not be paid. Clearly, there is a financial cost to discord when you are receiving public benefits.

Applicants for either benefit must be Canadian citizens or people resident in Canada after age 18 for at least 10 years prior to application.

The Guaranteed Income Supplement is paid to people who receive or who are qualified to receive Old Age Security. Due to a quirk in the regulations, the GIS can actually boost OAS payments. Here's how this works.

When you meet the qualification test for GIS, OAS payments below the full statutory amount payable to those resident in Canada for 40 years after age 18 are accelerated to the full amount, effectively wiping out the time penalty for those who do not meet the 40-year test. So by qualifying for GIS, the applicant winds up with full OAS and the appropriate amount of GIS.

When a person who receives the Spouse's Allowance or the Survivor's Allowance reaches age 65, those programs end and benefits shift to GIS.

Provincial Low-Income Supplementary Programs

Each province and territory has a series of programs that boost the disposable income of qualifying senior citizens. The programs include plans to reduce or eliminate expenses for prescription drugs, to reduce the cost of heating the home, to provide reduced fares for public transportation, and to reduce or eliminate fees for various government services.

A full description of these programs would fill an entire book. Rather than try to catalogue these services, I have listed phone numbers and web addresses for them. These websites and phone numbers are current as of the time this table has been written, but may change. For more specific references, use a web search engine for a suitable formulation of what you want, such as "Manitoba Pharmacare." You can also call directory assistance for your province or go to http://www.canada411.ca.

Province	Phone	Web address
B.C.	1-800-465-4911	http://www.cserv.gov.bc.ca/seniors/
Alberta	1-800-642-3853	http://www.gov.ab.ca
Saskatchewan	1- 877 800 0002	http://cr.gov.sk.ca/income-assistance/
Manitoba	1-800-665-6565	http://www.gov.mb.ca/shas/
Ontario	1-800-263-7965	http://www.gov.on.ca
Quebec	1-877-644-4545	http://www.gouv.qc.ca/portail/quebec/pgs/commun/?lang=en
New Brunswick	1-506-453-2001	http://www.gnb.ca/0017/Seniors/SeniorsGuide-e.pdf
Nova Scotia	1-902-424-0561	http://www.gov.ns.ca/scs/
Prince Edward Island	1-902-368-4930	http://www.gov.pe.ca/sss/index.php3

Newfoundland and Labrador	1-709-729-6507	http://www.health.gov.nl.ca/ health/nlpdp/plan_n.htm
Nunavut	see federal programs	
NWT		http://www.hlthss.gov.nt.ca/
Yukon	1-867-667-5674	http://www.hss.gov.yk.ca/programs/ social_services/seniors/

Application for GIS Benefits

To receive benefits, you must go through an application process that may ask for a marriage certificate from a religious institution in which a marriage took place or from a provincial registrar of vital statistics. Couples in same-sex relationships or living in common-law arrangements will be asked to sign a statutory declaration of that status.

The GIS is based on individual or combined incomes of spouses or qualifying partners. Because incomes change, the applicant must supply fresh income data each year. Failure to do the paperwork leads to a termination of benefits. GIS asks that it be told if a beneficiary marries or separates. However, if a separation occurs for a medical reason, such as hospitalization, benefits may continue.

The GIS benefit requires you to disclose all your income sources. Old Age Security benefits, GIS benefits, and the Spouse's Allowance are not considered income for the purpose of the GIS application. But other income has to be reported, including the following:

- CPP or QPP benefits
- Private or company pension income and superannuation
- Foreign pension income
- RRSP/RRIF payments
- Employment Insurance benefits

- Interest, capital gains, or dividends from investments
- Rental income
- Employment income
- Income from other sources such as workers' compensation

Canada Pension Plan

The Canada Pension Plan and its provincial counterpart, the Quebec Pension Plan, provide distributions of money to those who have qualified by paying into the system. Payments are structured to follow changes in the Consumer Price Index and may begin as early as age 60 or as late as age 70.

The core question about CPP/QPP is what it will pay. The theory is that it will pay a quarter of the average of each year's maximum pensionable earnings (YMPE) during working years with an indexation adjustment. YMPE is set to measure the average national wage, but the concept is loose. YMPE is based on wages or self-employed earnings. The period of contribution runs from 1966 for persons born before 1948 or the individual's 18th birthday if born after 1948. The YMPE accrual period extends to the earlier of the time CPP benefits begin to flow or to the individual's 70th birthday. It is possible to check with CPP for a statement of YMPEs by a phone call to 1-800-277-9914. For 2008, the YMPE for both the Canada and Quebec Pension Plans is $44,900. Directories of information about the CPP and QPP can be found at http://www1.servicecanada.gc.ca/en/isp/oas/ tabrates/tabmain. shtml and http://www.rrq.gouv.qc.ca/en/programmes/regime_ rentes/travail_cotisations/. CPP/QPP allows contributors to include their best years in the calculation of YMPE or, to put it differently, to exclude their lowest-income years. There is a broad provision for a 15 percent dropout in the contributory period. The same concept extends to periods of child rearing for children under seven years of age. The child-rearing dropout adds to the 15 percent dropout. The gender of the parent is not relevant, but both parents cannot obtain the child-rearing dropout for the same years. The parental dropout applies to CPP beneficiaries who were residents of Canada for tax purposes in the period beginning January 1, 1959. As well, for CPP/QPP calculations will exclude months during which the registrant received disability payments from the CPP/QPP system.

There is a balanced cost and benefit to drawing benefits before age 65—you may apply as of your 60th birthday provided you affirm that you are not working for a defined period—or as late as age 70. For each month prior to the applicant's 65th birthday, benefits are reduced by $^1/_2$ of 1 percent or 6 percent per year. For each month after the applicant's 65th birthday, benefits are increased by $^1/_2$ of 1 percent for a maximum of 6 percent per year. Benefits can be paid outside of Canada, though foreign jurisdictions may tax them. The maximum benefit at time of writing is $10,615 per year.

Early application for CPP/QPP benefits requires that you not be working by the end of the month before the retirement pension begins and during the month in which it begins. Thus, if you want your pension to start in June, you have to stop working by the end of May.

Alternatively, you can meet the test for qualification for early application for CPP/QPP if you earn less than the maximum CPP maximum retirement pension, which is $884.58 at time of writing in 2008, in the month prior to beginning the retirement pension and in the month in which the pension begins. Once the pension starts, you can go back to work. You need no longer contribute to CPP/QPP. If you change your mind and decide not to take CPP, you can cancel your retirement pension up to six months after it begins, but you must ask for the cancellation in writing. You must also pay back all the benefits you received and pay CPP contributions on any earnings while you were receiving the pension.

When you should begin to tap CPP/QPP benefits is a question that taxes the talents of experienced actuaries. Optimizing payouts requires that one estimate the following:

1. Cash flows: CPP/QPP payments at 65 compared to reduced flows before age 65 and increased flows after age 65
2. Timing: The effect of the three different scenarios or, for those who have spreadsheet skills, the effect of beginning CPP/QPP payments in any of the 120 monthly periods between ages 60 and 70
3. Income tax: The tax implications of maximum averaging starting at age 60 and allowing for the 30 percent reduction and shorter period averaging for periods after the 60th birthday, and
4. Clawback: The accelerated tax effects of various CPP/QPP flows for Old Age Security recipients close enough to the clawback point to suffer a loss of OAS by going over the trigger point, which is $64,718 at time of writing.

No two cases are alike, but we can make some general suggestions on how to handle the timing of CPP/QPP benefits.

1. For those who have retirement incomes other than CPP/QPP and OAS below $40,000 per year, tax and clawback issues are not important.
2. For those with net incomes excluding CPP/QPP over $105,000, the OAS clawback is certain. CPP/QPP benefits will not increase the odds of the clawback, for it will take all OAS benefits.

3. For those who are seriously ill and have diminished life expectancy, early application for CPP/QPP is wise.

Studies on CPP/QPP benefits timing tend to show that age 65 is a good time to start the flow of benefits. The reason is not just elimination of the $^1/_2$ of 1 percent per month penalty for each month prior to age 65 at which benefits begin, but the termination of the CPP/QPP employee tax for earned incomes. The tax is double for the self-employed. For the self-employed, therefore, it pays to make application as of the 60th birthday, provided that the work or income tests can be satisfied. On average, the tax saved will not be compensated by the additional benefits earned by waiting to begin benefits at age 65.

Deferral of benefits to age 70 provides a 30 percent boost to the monthly CPP/QPP age 65 payment, but the period of payment is theoretically shortened by death. However, we must note that people who have a high probability of living beyond age 90 are able to gain by postponement. It is cavalier to say that one should consult one's genes, but a family history of longevity is relevant to the benefit postponement decision. Women, with longer life expectancy than men, are better candidates to benefit from postponement of benefits.

QUESTION: What is the minimum qualifying age for retirement benefits payable by the Canada and Quebec Pension Plans?

ANSWER: Sixty-five, but benefits may begin with a penalty that works out to a 30 percent reduction of age 65 benefits at age 60 or as late as age 70 with a bonus equal to 30 percent of the age 65 benefits.

Here is a simple method of estimating what CPP/QPP will pay. It involves calculating benefits for various test retirement ages to ascertain the effect of accelerating or delaying CPP/QPP benefits.

For retirement before age 65:

1. Pension at age 65 per CPP
   or QPP statements   _____
2. Number of months of retirement
   before age 65   _____
3. Line 2 times 0.5   _____
4. Pension reduction (line 1 × line 3) _____
5. Net pension (line 1 minus line 4)   _____

For retirement after age 65:

1. Pension at age 65 per CPP/QPP statements   _____
2. Number of months benefits postponed   _____
3. Line 2 times 0.5   _____
4. Pension increase (line 1 × line 2)   _____
5. Net pension (line 1 plus line 4)   _____

These are calculations of nominal benefits. We should estimate the opportunity cost of early application by adding a sum equal to what that money could earn if invested. We have also ignored compounding of these opportunity returns. But these additions to the basic estimates can be ignored. After all, if you spend the money you get from CPP or QPP, there is nothing to invest. In any event, what money could have earned is speculative. Those with a taste for rigorous analysis can do it, but the exercise is more academic than essential.

There is, nevertheless, a pension gap. If we include taxation, the gap closes substantially, for every year you remain in the CPP/QPP system, there is a charge on wages equal to 0.0495 percent of qualifying income up to the Year's Maximum Pensionable Earnings (currently $44,900) less the charge on a $3,500 exemption that has been in effect since 1997. Those who are self-employed pay double the rate or 9.9 percent of income up to YMPE. However, if our person were to be in a lower tax bracket in retirement, if tax rates decline in future, or if his or her average annual YMPE were to rise appreciably via five years of additional work, the advantage or disadvantage of early or late retirement would change.

Death and Other Benefits

CPP and QPP benefits extend to payment of death benefits—a maximum of $2,500 payable to the person who paid for the funeral of the CPP beneficiary.

Disability is a condition deemed by the Medical Adjudicator of the Canada Pension Plan or the Quebec Pension Plan to be severe and prolonged. Severe means that the person can have no gainful employment. Prolonged means a situation in which the contributor cannot return to work in the near future. Each case is assessed on an individual basis. The maximum disability payment as of January 2008 is $1,077 per month. The actual payment depends on the opinion of the Medical Adjudicator and of the amount of CPP contributions that were made. QPP has a similar arrangement.

CPP and OAS benefits are indexed to rise with the so-called headline number, which is the all-inclusive number, of the Consumer Price Index. This is a vital feature of Canada's national pension system, for most employment pensions, other than defined benefit plans, do not have cost of living indexation.

Canada's current rate of inflation is between 2.0 and 2.5 percent a year, which is moderate on a world scale. The loonie is currently sound because Canada is the only G-7 country with a declining government deficit and a positive balance of trade. Other countries may have higher rates of inflation, and high inflation rates tend to reduce the value of currencies. Therefore, CPP/QPP beneficiaries in countries with high inflation rates will see the purchasing power of CPP/QPP payments and OAS benefits as well as other payments in Canadian dollars rise in local value. However, payments made to recipients outside of Canada have a 25 percent withholding tax applied unless the country has a tax treaty with Canada.

Although you will hear the idea floated that government pension plans are not here to stay, both the Canadian plans are well funded according to actuarial assumptions.

Payments of Benefits Abroad

Subject to tax treaties, withholding of income tax from CPP benefits begins the month after CPP is notified that the beneficiary is out of Canada with the intent of living outside of Canada. CPP presumes intent from a foreign address. Therefore, a beneficiary should take care to retain a Canadian address for short trips out of the country. Naturally, it would be appropriate to advise CPP or QPP of a genuine intent to leave Canada for extended periods. Contact the Canada Revenue Agency or the Régie des rentes du Québec for more information on withholding in respect of foreign countries.

A list of countries and withholding rates is available at the Canada Revenue Agency website at http://www.cra.gc.ca; search for "ic76-12r6." Then open the PDF as indicated and search for the country and the withholding rate of concern. Alternatively, you can call the CRA International Tax Office, non-resident withholding division, at 800-267-3395.

The taxation of benefits is a web of complexity. Retirement, disability, and survivor payments have the peculiar characteristic of triggering high tax rates on people who receive various income supplements such as GIS. It seems to be a case of robbing Peter to pay Paul. As well, through what are called bridging provisions, employer-paid pension plans will often reduce their payouts as CPP payments come on stream at age 65.

CPP/QPP benefits are deferred income based on employment and self-employment. CPP/QPP can be divided either by a voluntary process for tax savings or by splitting upon divorce or separation. In this section, we'll discuss the CPP view of splitting on divorce or separation. If either partner has never worked outside of Quebec, then it is necessary to contact the Régie des rentes du Québec for information. Call 1-800-463-5185 or 1-418-643-5185 or go to http://www.rrq.gouv.qc.ca.

The voluntary form of pension splitting allows couples who are married or equivalent to married to partition their CPP/QPP benefits provided that both are at least 60 years of age and have applied for or are already receiving CPP/QPP benefits.

The process of splitting requires a Social Insurance Number and a marriage certificate or proof of a common-law relationship. The splitting process, once in effect, runs until separation or divorce or the death of one partner. The splitting arrangement can also be cancelled by request of both parties.

Involuntary splitting upon separation or divorce divides entitlements on a 50/50 basis for the time of the marriage, but there are quirks in the process. If one spouse had no employment during the time of the marriage, then a swap of partner A's benefits to partner B will produce a lopsided result, for A, who may be the principal breadwinner, makes a substantial transfer to B, who earned nothing, while B gives nothing to A. If B goes to work, she, and it is usually a she, can exclude her zero income years and wind up boosted to the maximum payout.

Several provinces allow couples to elect not to split. In any case, it is useful for couples splitting up to define who gets what, including CPP benefits, in an agreement. There is no telling what courts may do with these agreements in future. Either side may initiate a split, and joint consent is not required except in Quebec, where equivalent-to-married arrangements do require joint consent. CPP judges an equivalent-to-married relationship to exist after a year of cohabitation. Quebec insists on three years but one year is enough if there is a child of the union or an adoption.

Chapter Summary

There are four levels of the pension system in Canada. Three are based on private savings, investments, or corporate pension plans. Only one level, public pensions, is available to persons resident in Canada who have met certain tests for living in Canada and paying into the Canada Pension Plan or the Quebec Pension Plan. Old Age Security is, in general, paid to residents of Canada who are 65 years of age. Benefits may be reduced by the clawback. For people whose income is below a web of limits that varies with single/ married or equivalent-to-married status and income, the Guaranteed Income Supplement may also be paid. Provincial programs may enhance the GIS supplement. The Canada and Quebec Pension Plans are targeted to start at age 65 but benefits may begin as early as age 60 or as late as age 70. For every month before age 65 that benefits begin, benefits are reduced by 0.5 percent per month for each month before age 65. For persons beginning benefits after the 65th birthday, benefits are increased by 0.5 percent per month for each month after the 65th birthday that benefits begin.

Chapter 6

Where Will the Money Come From? Employment and Private Pension Sources

The variety of employment pensions can be bewildering. You will find defined benefit plans that generate predictable payments, defined contribution plans that leave it up to the contributor to make investment decisions, various group Registered Retirement Savings Plans that are much the same as conventional RRSPs but with the advantage of what are usually lower management fees and commissions, deferred profit-sharing plans run by employers for the benefit of employees, and the Quebec variation—the Member Funded Pension Plan or MFPP, created in 2006, a blend of the defined benefit plan, which makes predictable payouts, and the defined contribution plan, which lets employers avoid having to worry about being liable for plan deficits. In this chapter, we'll review the rules for company pension plans. Rules change, so you should check with the Canada Revenue Agency or your own tax professional to determine the status of applicable regulations.

Defined Benefit Plans

The defined benefit pension or DB plan provides the model for what people still often think a pension should be. This type of pension is a deferred wage used to buy what amounts to an annuity or income flow for the life of the retiree. There can also be additional benefits for defined survivors. Many defined benefits plans are indexed to change in the Consumer Price Index as well.

DB plans have become scarce over the years. The costs of funding them during the high inflation period from 1973 to 1982 and the decline of union contracts in major industries together with the cost of complying with complex regulations have led employers to wash their hands of these devices in favour of defined contribution plans that promise nothing at all in the future.

From an employer's point of view, DB plans are costly and of uncertain value. They need to be funded sufficiently well to provide deferred compensation in the future. How well depends on the opinions of actuaries—mathematicians who work in the field of risk. Actuarial projections change with interest rates and expected numbers of people who will draw pensions. If beneficiaries live longer than expected when the plan was created, employers must come up with extra cash to fund benefits. On the other hand, if the plans run surpluses because of gains in fund investments or because there are fewer survivors who will qualify for pensions, they may be raided by employers. Many DB plans run perpetual deficits, which tends not to be a problem as long as companies have the cash to top them up when necessary.[1]

DB plans come in two flavours. In non-contributory plans, the employers handle all funding and the employees need contribute nothing. In contributory plans, future beneficiaries of the plans must contribute during their working years. Many DB plans link to the Canada and Quebec Pension Plans and have bridge provisions that allow early retirees to get a stipulated pension that is then reduced when the CPP/QPP benefits begin to flow at age 65.

Figuring out what a DB plan will pay requires the beneficiary to determine how the benefits are calculated. Some measure the career average earnings; more commonly the final several years of earnings or even the final 10 years of earnings before retirement are measured. Some plans use a measure of best years. Each beneficiary has to check with the company's pension administrator or human resources department to determine what to expect.

Some plans have generous bridge benefits to the time that benefits from the Canada or Quebec Pension Plans begin. The bridge provides temporary income that may actually exceed CPP/QPP benefits at age 65. Where a bridge plan exists, it pays a sum that ends at age 65, the standard start point for CPP/QPP. Even if a DB plan has no bridge provision, an employee may be able to achieve something similar by asking the employer to pay more up to age 65 and less later. Some plans permit this.

A desire for fairness in defined benefit pension plans has bred complexity. Some of the plans, especially those in very large companies, raise their pension bases in order to compensate for inflation. The rationale for this is that an employee who started in, say, 1970 and whose career earnings will be averaged will actually be penalized for his loyalty. The wage that was respectable and even desirable nearly four decades ago, and on which the pension is based, is ridiculously low today. Without an inflation adjustment, the employee will be paying the cost of inflation by way of an eroded payout. Deferred wage compensation is a fair modification of the concept of the deferred wage that underlies all pensions.

The same concept of fairness underlies multi-employer pension plans that attempt, through union agreements, to ensure that workers will get recognition for going from one job to another, usually with a different employer. Typically, these plans pay a flat sum for each year of membership or service. The plans have proliferated and produced variations by job category or wage level and for time period, such as decade or interval of years, of service. These plans are subject to the same solvency tests as other defined benefit plans. If there is not enough money in the plan to meet actuarial tests for solvency, the plans may cut their benefits or, if they lose a great deal of money on their investments, even have to be wound up.

There are egregious cases of defined benefit pension plans being axed by employers. Long-term disability is a form of a defined benefit plan, one linked to a condition rather than to an age. The following story of one plan deserves to be remembered:

When the T. Eaton Company shut down operations in 1999, employees who had been receiving benefits for injuries on the job lost their income source. They were members of the company's Long Term Disability Plan (LTD for short), which was self-financed by Eaton's. The plan was also underfunded. It lacked sufficient capital to run without cash injections from the company. When Eaton's filed for protection under the Companies Creditors Arrangement Act (CCAA), its disability plan ceased to exist. The disability plan was legal and proper, for self-insured plans did not need to be fully funded to actuarial standards.

The failure of the Eaton plan left people with terminal illnesses, AIDS, cancer, and other serious conditions and disabilities on their own. Some could draw on CPP disability benefits, which vary with contributions. But many Eaton employees, especially those who did not qualify for CPP or who did not get sufficient benefits from CPP, were forced to go on welfare. It could have been avoided. Indeed, in 1995, Eaton's own benefits managers went to upper management and asked to have the LTD plan funded. They were turned down.

Eaton's chose to carry the liability for these benefits. It did not have to post the liability on its balance sheet and, in any case, it was for most of its history a private company. The liability might better have been shifted to an insurance company, but Eaton's chose not to spend money buying coverage. Eaton's walked away from this cost, which left employees who had been expecting lifelong support to find other resources. Most, especially the severely injured and the elderly, could not.[2]

The moral of the T. Eaton & Co. story is that it is essential for those with a stake in pensions to read mail from their employers and its pension sponsors about the plans. Underfunding of a long-term undertaking, which was extreme in the Eaton's LTD case, happens often but is not necessarily serious. If a company has the cash flow to maintain pension payments through supplemental injections of cash out of operating earnings, the problem may be relatively minor. Clearly, in the Eaton's case, the problem was major. An insolvent company could not continue to make payments, after all.

Most DB plans in Canada are operated by governments and Crown corporations and are therefore substantially immune from the funding issues that can challenge plans run by ordinary businesses. Crown corporations tend to be monopolies like Canada Post Corp., which has no competitors for first-class mail. They are able to use that monopoly power to ensure that pension obligations are met.

According to a report by management consultancy Watson Wyatt, the average DB pension plan in Canada is fully funded. The typical pension fund ratio—the level of assets compared to the level of liabilities—rose to over 100 percent in the second quarter of 2007. Strong stock market returns are responsible for the increased security of pension funds.[3]

Individual Pension Plans: The Concept of Defined Contributions

The pension systems of Canada and the United States have been moving away from defined benefit plans toward defined contribution plans. The reasons are strictly financial, for an employer's costs and responsibilities tend to be much less with defined contribution plans.

The reduction in the responsibility of employers has a counterpoint in the increased responsibility of employees and the self-employed to invest their money wisely. In defined contribution plans, the employer may select a plan administrator and offer a guide to the procedures for making investment decisions. The plans, sometimes referred to as "capital accumulation plans," leave the responsibility for investments with members.

There are three basic types of employer-sponsored plans:

1. deferred profit-sharing plans,
2. group RRSPs, and
3. defined contribution registered pension plans.

Each has distinct advantages and complications.

1. *Deferred Profit-Sharing Plans* require the employer to make all contributions. Employers may contribute as they can or wish

without having to contribute every year. Employers can as well take their money out if the employee leaves before the end of a two-year period after joining the plan. After that, all contributions vest, that is, become the employee's money. These plans are sometimes used by small companies as a way to distribute some of their own shares to employees. The biggest advantage for the employee is that withdrawals can be made in a lump sum and need not be removed over a period of years, as they would be in various styles of RRSPs. As well, the employee can take as long as 10 years to take money out.

2. *Group RRSPs* have become a substitute for other pension plans, such as defined benefit plans, that employers used to offer. Group RRSPs have the appearance of company pension plans, but they are really individual plans dressed up in the clothes of a company plan. Participation in these plans can be pushed by the employer or left to employees' preferences. Employers can contribute to employees' accounts, but, in a technical sense, each RRSP is individual. Thus a group RRSP is a collection of individual plans with one structure and administrator. Participation may be left to the choice of the employee or, where the employer adds to the employee's account, it may be like a DB plan in which the employer provides some contributions.

A distinct advantage of group RRSPs is fee efficiency. If a plan administrator or trustee offers a large cut on management fees or has a number of mutual funds with good track records in bull and bear markets, it may be worth joining. Employees can direct payroll deductions to the plan.

Some employers may use their company's RRSP as a quasi-defined contribution plan and match employee contributions. Money contributed is regarded as the employee's own and can be taken out any time without conditions about years of service or age. Group RRSPs exist in a regulatory vacuum in some provinces, for in spite of their outward similarity to conventional defined contribution pension plans, they have been excluded from provincial pension regulation in New Brunswick, Saskatchewan, and British Columbia.[4]

3. *Defined Contribution Registered Pension Plans (DCRPPs)* are plans like RRSPs but with a few differences. With RRSPs, there is no need to make periodic contributions. You can put money in one year and then skip a year or two or just never contribute again. But with DCRPPs, the employer has to add money each year. Typically, it may be 5 percent of qualifying earnings. Depending on the plan, employees may also be required to contribute each year.

The problem with DCRPPs is the relatively rigid framework of regulation covering what the retiree may do with the money. In many cases, an annuity must be purchased with funds in the DCRPP. In other cases, the plan may permit the retiree to roll funds into a Locked-In Retirement Account (LIRA), a Locked-In Retirement Income Fund (LRIF), or a Life Income Fund (LIF).

Each of these alternatives has a paternalistic motive behind the legislation. The various plans and the annuity alternative all regulate what the employee can take out. The notion is that no one in the plan will be able to exhaust the funds. Of course, for those with other assets, who have life insurance, perhaps annuities, and so on, the plans are burdensome and can even create tax problems if, for example, they force the employee into a higher income bracket or push income high enough for Old Age Security benefits to be clawed back in whole or in part. A growing number of provinces allow early withdrawals from certain locked-in plans, but they do so with daunting amounts of paperwork.

QUESTION: What are the differences between defined benefit and defined contribution pension plans with regard to funding sources and future income?

ANSWER: Defined benefit plans are funded mainly by employers and offer predictable payouts. Defined contribution pension plans are funded mainly by employees and leave it up to contributors to manage investments.

Registered Retirement Savings Plans

The concept of the Registered Retirement Savings Plan is utter simplicity. Folks who put some of their income into an RRSP and get a tax deduction for qualifying contributions wind up having the income taxed when it is received rather than when it is earned.

That time gap constitutes much of the appeal of RRSPs, for the money that is earned within RRSPs is not taxed until distribution. That allows for potential decades of tax-free growth. The downside of RRSPs is that all money that comes out is subject to tax as income at whatever marginal rates are applicable at the time of withdrawal. The distributions from RRSPs do not qualify for preferential treatment at lower tax rates, as do dividends and capital gains. Moreover, RRSP distributions in any form, whether lump sum, annuity, or via Registered Retirement Income Funds, will raise net income and may, thereby, expose Old Age Security payments to the OAS clawback.

RRSPs, invented in the government of Prime Minister Louis St. Laurent in 1957, are more than 50 years old. They have progressed from being obscure to being the most common of investment devices for the employed and the self-employed.

Tax-free accumulation is possible in a variety of other ways— through earnings retention in private corporations, for example; through Registered Education Savings Plans; and through Tax-Free Savings Accounts, which were introduced in the February 2008 federal budget. The virtue of the RRSP is that, in the pension world, it is democratic. It is a way for self-employed people to generate pensions that were formerly restricted to employees of companies or governments that had plans.

There is also an immediate tax advantage to making RRSP contributions, for the money that goes in each year is, within prescribed limits, eliminated from taxable income in the year earned.

The tax incentive for contributions grows with the individual's marginal tax rate, thus there is more for the high income earner to gain from RRSPs than for the lower income earner.

RRSP contribution limits have risen over the years. For 2008, the limit is the lesser of 20 percent of the prior year's qualifying income, or $20,000. The limit will rise to $21,000 for 2009, $22,000 for 2010. After that, the limit will be indexed for inflation.[5]

To calculate how much you can contribute to your RRSP, subtract what you have paid into the employer's pension fund from your RRSP limit. The amount that must be deducted is called the pension adjustment, or PA.

The more that the employee or the employer sets aside in a DB or DC pension, the less that may be contributed to an RRSP. If a person is not a member of a company pension plan, a government plan, or a deferred profit-sharing plan, the pension adjustment is zero and the contributions to the respective year's RRSP limit can be put into the RRSP.

The RRSP limit may be reduced by a past service pension adjustment (PSPA). That happens if pension benefits under a DB plan are enhanced retroactively by an employer. Then, if the employee leaves the company before retirement, it may be possible to obtain a pension adjustment reversal, PAR for short. The PAR gives back some of the RRSP contribution space lost because of the pension adjustment while the person was in the company pension plan.[6]

There used to be time limits for contributions to RRSPs, but the concept of the deadline has withered. In the past if you did not make a contribution by a certain date, you lost out on the ability to make up that amount. However, now, unused capacity for contributions in RRSPs is carried forward using the idea of "RRSP room." But there remains a deadline for deductions. Contributions still have to be made in the calendar year to which they are to be applied or in the first 60 days of the following calendar year.

The many vendors of mutual funds have made it a custom to say that one should contribute as early as possible each year. They have charts to show that the money that builds up at a constant rate of return will be greater if you make earlier contributions rather than deferring the contributions until year end. That is true, but markets have moods. Experienced investors can do well to avoid investing at what seems to be market tops and to try to wait for bottoms to make further investments.

The first 60 days of each year are a special period in which money contributed may be allocated either to the year past or the new year. Some financial advisors advocate overcontributing by as much as $2,000, which is a cumulative limit. It exists to help people cope with the pension adjustment, that is, money contributed to a qualifying pension, typically through employment.

Overcontributions generate tax-free compounding, but if you exceed the $2,000 cumulative limit, you will be charged a penalty of 1 percent per month until the excess contribution is withdrawn or used up in the next or successive years. Even within the $2,000 limit, sums contributed over the annual limit do not generate tax savings. You are really contributing after-tax dollars. That means the money will have been taxed twice—once when earned and once more when paid out. Carrying an excess contribution of $2,000 or less to an RRSP is not a major problem, but you should be careful to use it up in the last year of eligibility.

What to Do with Your RRSP

There are three things to be done with RRSP accumulations, and you must choose one of them to implement no later than the end of the year in which you turn 71. By that time, the RRSP balance must be taken out in a lump sum, used to purchase an annuity, or converted to a Registered Retirement Income Fund. If you have a younger spouse or equivalent to spouse, though, you can contribute to your spouse's RRSP until the end of the year in which the spouse turns 71.

Taking a Lump Sum

Taking money as a lump sum exposes it to full marginal taxation. This is the least attractive and certainly the least tax-efficient way to get money for retirement. The money taken out is taxed as ordinary income, and even if some of the money in the RRSP has been generated by capital gains that might in part or whole be tax-exempt, the money is considered income. Moreover, a portion of the amount taken out of the RRSP will be withheld at source by the financial institution and sent to the Canada Revenue Agency or Revenu Québec. You have to report the income and the sums withheld on your annual income tax return. If not enough money was withheld by the financial institution, you have to pay additional tax.

Taking money as an annuity can be useful. A life annuity ensures that the beneficiary can never run out of money. But if you have several other pensions, it may be unwise or unnecessary to add yet another. An annuity loses intrinsic value if interest rates rise substantially after its purchase. OAS and CPP are annuities in form, but they are superior to most private annuities, which are not indexed, in that they raise their payments as the cost of living rises. The RRSP proceeds that produce annuity income are not taxed until they are received. As well, up to $2,000 per year of income can be exempted through the use of the pension income credit.[7]

Annuities

There are three general kinds of annuities, any one of which can be adjusted to the needs of the person receiving the money.

A term certain annuity pays income to the annuitant or to his or her estate for a fixed number of years so that, if an annuitant dies very soon after purchasing the annuity, money can continue to flow to another designated beneficiary such as a spouse. A single life or life annuity pays money to just the annuitant for as long as he or she is alive. A joint and last survivor annuity pays income until the death of the last spouse or partner.

Annuities are sold by insurance companies and it is vital to make sure that the company you choose is financially solid. Large insur-

QUESTION: What can an annuity do that a lump sum payout or a RRIF cannot do? What is the downside of an annuity?

ANSWER: Annuities ensure that the annuitant can never run out of money. But in exchange for that guarantee, the payouts are fixed and do not rise with inflation. Annuities are certain but inflexible, unlike RRIFs, which are flexible but uncertain.

ance companies can go bust—witness the collapse of Confederation Life in 1994, just a year after it received excellent marks from insurance company rating agencies. Confederation Life's demise can be attributed to its ignoring a fundamental rule of investing: Diversify. Just as large companies need to diversify in their investments, so should the potential retiree—and that applies to annuities too. Don't put all your annuity eggs in one basket. Many of its obligations were picked up by Assuris, formerly called CompCorp, the short name of the Canadian Life and Health Compensation Corporation.

It's useful to understand what took Confederation Life from its position in 1993, when it was the fourth largest life insurance company in Canada, to insolvency. The culprit was Confederation's vast commitment of assets to real estate. It went from having just $119,000 in property investments in 1982 to $1.1 billion in real estate by August 1994. Likewise, its mortgage holdings went from $1.2 billion in 1982 to $8.5 billion by 1993. It had put 71 percent of its assets into real estate in the form of mortgages, condos, shopping malls, and houses.

Riding a property boom worked out well as interest rates fell and capital went looking for high returns. But when real estate values began to slump in 1993, its relatively undiversified portfolios lost money very quickly.[8]

Investigators found that Confederation had issued mortgages to speculative buyers who had put down as little as $1,000. Senior management had been resolute in its faith in real estate. The problems at the company were deep and intractable.

CompCorp covered most of the losses, indeed, 90 percent of policy holders were under the rescue fund's limits. Larger insurance contracts and annuities suffered reduced payments and the entire life insurance industry wound up paying some of Confederation's losses.

The ultimate lesson of Confederation Life is just this: Diversify. Do not put all your annuity eggs in one basket. It was not the first real estate empire gone bust nor will it be the last.

RRIFs and Other Self-Administered Plans

The final device for taking money out of RRSPs is the use of the Registered Retirement Income Fund or RRIF. RRIFs are distribution devices for money held in RRSPs. You can take out money at any time, but once an RRSP has been converted to a RRIF, no more RRSP contributions can be made to that plan—the RRSP no longer exists. Other RRSPs that have not been converted to RRIFs can continue to receive contributions providing the usual RRSP conditions are met. A RRIF can be left in your will for a spouse or other beneficiary. It is also flexible, for while there are prescribed minimums for withdrawals, there are no maximum limits on how much can be taken out.

Some RRIF income can be exempted from taxation through the pension income tax credit, up to a limit of $2,000 or $1,000 in

Quebec.[9] The amounts that must be taken out of the RRIF rise each year from a few percent at age 71 to age 94, at which you must take out 20 percent of the remaining value of the RRIF each year. However, RRIF rules allow the age of the spouse to be used in determining minimum withdrawals. If the spouse is younger, then you may extend the tax deferral. Withdrawals must begin in the year after the year in which you turn 71. In that year, you have to take out 7.38 percent of the RRIF balance. However, once a RRIF is created, withdrawals must begin. Before age 71, the minimum withdrawal required is the sum of money in the RRIF divided by 90 less your age at the time.

At death, the entire amount of funds held in RRIFs and RRSPs are deemed to be converted to income. But if the funds are left to the taxpayer's spouse or to a financially dependent child, they should be included in the income of the spouse or child.

Locked-In Plans

Depending on the jurisdiction in which one has been employed, it is possible to unlock funds in locked-in plans. If covered by existing provincial rules, then provincial rules apply. But if a pension plan is of an organization regulated by the federal government, such as chartered banks, then federal unlocking rules apply. It is the jurisdiction that counts. Most plans are covered by provincial rules, but for guidance, one must know the legislation.

Under certain pension rules, you can be prevented from withdrawing pension benefits from an employer's plan when you leave a company. The rules require that money taken out of such a plan be put into a Locked-In Retirement Account or LIRA. The rules governing LIRAs are complex, to say the least. They often stipulate that you can use plan funds only to buy an annuity or special RRIF, which is then called a Life Income Fund (LIF) or a Life Retirement Income Fund (LRIF). Where pension legislation allows a shift from a registered pension plan to a locked-in RRSP, LIF, or LRIF, no taxes are to be paid on the transferred funds, though the sums that can be transferred may be limited.

A LIF is a RRIF for tax purposes. Minimum amounts can be taken out each year, as with RRIFs. But LIFs impose maximum amounts that can be taken out. This is a serious disadvantage, not least because it assumes that beneficiaries are spendthrifts who cannot be trusted to look after their own money. In some provinces, funds remaining in a LIF must be used to buy a life annuity by December 31 of the year in which the person turns 80. However, with LRIFs, there is no need to buy an annuity at age 80 and the maximums for withdrawals may be flexible. This is an active area of reform, so check with a tax advisor to determine your choices. For now, in provinces that allow both LRIFs and LIFs, it is possible to start with a LIF and then shift money to a LRIF if you want to avoid the necessity of buying an annuity. The strategy is sensible. After all, a LIF offers more flexible withdrawal rates with higher maximums than are available for LRIFs. LIFs allow for withdrawal of capital. LRIFs allow only for the removal of earnings.

There is growing recognition that there can be something fundamentally unfair about holding people's money when they have a good need for it. The provinces have adopted various methods for unlocking funds in locked-in plans. For example, Saskatchewan initiated a process of replacing locked-up funds in LRIFs and LIFs with a so-called prescribed RRIF that has no maximum withdrawal limits or required annuity purchase. This "PRIF" works like a regular RRIF with minimum withdrawals each year based on the age of the contributor or spouse. Manitoba adopted a variation of the concept of the PRIF. In Manitoba, you can take out up to half the value of a LIF or LRIF and put that money into a PRIF provided that the transfer is approved by a current partner, that the transferor is at least 55 years old, that the transfer is approved by former spouses, and that it does not interfere with family support obligations. The plan came with a great deal of bureaucratic baggage. Ontario adopted a procedure for unlocking 25 percent of the value of certain locked in-plans as of January 1, 2008.[10]

In May 2008, the federal government caught up to provincial law and adopted national unlocking rules that allow individuals who have funds in locked-in RRSPs and life income funds in the pension funds of federally chartered organizations such as banks and other entities to have access to their money. Those persons can now obtain funds from LIFS in three cases; small balances, financial hardship, and a one-time 50 percent unlocking for no greater reason than one wants access to money.

The new federal rules are complex. Individuals must be a) 55 years of age or older, b) have RRSPs and LIFs less than the small balance limit of $22,450 (in 2008), or c) have a financial hardship such as job loss or medical or disability expenses. Persons at age 55 can just take half their balances and cash them out or transfer them to other institutions. Hardship will be an allowable cause for unlocking assets up to the $22,450 limit.[11]

What's best in this welter of plan designs and options? Large lump sums may expose the beneficiary to voluntary taxation on sums withdrawn. The risk is greatest for a middle-income, middle-tax-bracket beneficiary. The risk is low for a person with a low income who is withdrawing small sums.

For a taxpayer already in a top bracket and unable to reduce taxes for the rest of his or her life—perhaps the result of having a substantial investment income—the lump sum may do little harm. All money earned or received from registered plans is going to be taxed at peak rates anyway. Indeed, there may then be chances to reinvest the money in forms that produce tax-advantaged income like dividends or capital gains. The remaining choices are the annuity or the RRIF. The RRIF and its variations allow for management of assets that produce income. RRIFs can be destroyed by poor management, but they can also be managed to pace inflation—something that most annuities cannot do. Locked-in plans are intended to inhibit retired people from financial foolishness. But these plans can be self-directed and thus gutted by poor or unfortunate investment decisions.

The complexity of choices, the amounts of money involved, and the potential finality of decisions should be examined with the assistance of a tax advisor and a financial planner. Especially in cases where retirement income is limited, it is vital to find the right combination of convenience, security, income, and flexibility.

Tax-Free Savings Accounts

The February 26, 2008, federal budget contained a savings device that will be a valuable part of retirement savings. These accounts, called Tax-Free Savings Accounts (TFSAs), allow people over 18 years of age who have a Social Insurance Number and reside in Canada to deposit up to $5,000 per year in them. If you contribute nothing or less than the maximum, these amounts are carried forward as unused space. The amounts deposited will provide no up-front tax reduction, as RRSPs do, but will be allowed to grow without tax and to be paid out without tax of any kind assessed on the withdrawals. The accounting for periodic growth will exclude the sums realized within TFSA plans from income and therefore not increase the liability to suffer reductions of Old Age Security payments by the clawback. The money in TFSAs will be tax-paid and not represent tax liabilities. The TFSA will therefore not boost income and increase exposure to the OAS clawback. Nor will there be any age limits on the use of TFSAs.[12]

Think of Tax-Free Savings Accounts as neutral envelopes in which to deposit assets, within the maximum annual guideline. Interest income, taxed at the highest marginal rate, will escape tax altogether within TFSAs. There will be no minimum or maximum annual withdrawals nor any tax consequence for withdrawals. And there will be no contribution limit other than the cumulative value of $5,000 per year times the number of years from 2009 forward or the age to which TFSAs may be held. All this will make them vital accounts for retirement planning.

In planning for retirement, TFSAs and RRSPs come out about equal if you assume a similar return on invested assets in either plan and the same tax rate in both plans in contribution years and withdrawal years. With these assumptions, the choice of plan is tax-neutral. Note that RRSPs have to be funded out of earned income. TFSAs, on the other hand, can be funded with any income from rents, interest, dividends, wages, or capital gains. When compared to RRSPs, the tax breaks on TFSAs will be equal. The reasons are obvious. For any given tax rate and gross sum of money, the TFSA will start with a smaller net amount (tax has been deducted, after all). The RRSP will start with tax-free money but face taxation of income at the end.[13] But note that contributions to RRSPs produce taxable income when withdrawn. The income at withdrawal will boost net income and therefore increase the risk of erosion of Old Age Security by the clawback. The TFSA, which produces no taxable income at the end, will not increase income for purposes of the clawback. Moreover, if your tax bracket is rising over time with promotions, the TFSA will be the better choice. Indeed, if you have been prudent or lucky with investments, your retirement income could be higher than the income you earned early in your career. Thus you would face higher tax brackets in retirement than in working years. The RRSP will expose you to higher taxes, which is a perverse result. However, taxpayers in working years should use both RRSPs and TFSAs if there is sufficient money to fund both plans to the applicable limits. Moreover, in retirement, the TFSA will be the only plan available.

Chapter Summary

Employer and individual pension plans come in two basic varieties: defined benefit plans that are funded mainly by the employer, and defined contribution plans that are funded mainly by the employee or the individual. DB plans are less common than they used to be, for employers have elected to save money by transferring the duty to invest to beneficiaries. This is a tradeoff of certainty for flexibility. The same relationship exists in payout arrangements. You may use an annuity, which provides absolutely certain income for life but does not have any way to keep up with inflation, or a Registered Retirement Savings Plan, which has no certainty of payment but which can, if wisely invested and distributed through a Registered Retirement Income Fund, keep up with inflation or even beat it. The alphabet of locked-in RRSPs and RRIFs maintain this relationship, for they set formulas for payouts, putting caps on what basic RRIFs can pay, with the result that plan beneficiaries have assured money for life or at least into very old age, but limiting the beneficiary's ability to manage his or her own money. Amendments to locking-in rules now allow individuals access to at least some of their registered savings, subject to rule that vary by jurisdiction. The Tax-Free Savings Account, an innovation in 2009, will allow $5,000 per year of tax-paid money to be invested and accumulated with few strings and no further taxes. TFSAs start with less money out of any given amount of taxable earned income but create no tax liability at payout, unlike RRSPs, which impose a tax liability at payout in exchange for a tax holiday for contributions. TFSAs will have a valuable place in the web of pension plans.

Chapter 6 Appendix

Worksheets for Estimating Pension Income

This appendix provides a method for estimating retirement income from many sources. We begin with public pensions and then move to work-related and private pension plans such as RRSPs. Note that OAS and GIS rates are adjusted quarterly.

I. Public Pensions

Public pensions are made up of Old Age Security and the Guaranteed Income Supplement, the Canada Pension Plan and its partner, the Quebec Pension Plan.

Estimate the Old Age Security Clawback

Anticipated retirement income in 2008 dollars	$_____	a
Deduct OAS clawback start point for 2008	$ 64,718	b
Result: If 0 or negative, clawback does not apply	$_____	c
Clawback amount: (line c) times 0.15	$_____	d
Note that OAS is 100% reduced by the		
Clawback at $105,000 net income	$105,000	e
Retained Old Age Security:	$	
Full OAS benefit for Fall, 2008	$ 6,204	f
Partial pension: qualifying years	_____	g
Line f times 0.025	_____	h
Partial OAS: line h times line f	_____	i
OAS payable	$ _____	j

Apply line f if qualified for full pension or line j if qualified for partial OAS.

> Note that those who have lived in Canada for less than 40 years or who do not have 10 consecutive years of residence in Canada after age 18 or who were born before July 1, 1952, have a special rule to apply on an accelerated basis if they lived in Canada for six years after age 18. There are special procedures: Visit http://www.hrsdc.gc.ca/en/isp/pub/oas/oas.shtml or call 1-800-277-9914 for more information.

Estimate the Guaranteed Income Supplement

The Guaranteed Income Supplement is paid to people whose annual income, excluding OAS, GIS, and the Spouse's Allowance, is in a defined range. The maximum amount, payable to single, widowed, or divorced pensioners over age 65 who have no income other than OAS, GIS, and the Allowance, is $638.46 per month in the third quarter of 2008. The GIS amount payable declines as income rises and is zero at a yearly income excluding OAS, GIS, and the Spouse's Allowance of $15,336.

For persons over 65 who are married or living as common-law partners, who have no income other than OAS, GIS, and the Spouse's Allowance, and who are married to persons between the ages of 60 and 65, the Guaranteed Income Supplement begins at $421.62 per person per month in the third quarter of 2008 and declines to zero when income other than OAS, GIS, and the Spouse's Allowance reaches $20,256.

A quick calculator of GIS benefits can be found online at the Service Canada website: http://www1.servicecanada.gc.ca/en/isp/oas/tabrates/tabmain.shtml.

The calculator takes eligible income, which excludes OAS, GIS, and the Spouse's Allowance, then reduces GIS payable from the maximum amount at a rate of $1 of GIS benefit for $2 of income. For married people or those in common-law relationships, the deduction is $1 for every $4 of other income.

II. Employment Pensions

Employment-based pensions are made up of defined benefit and defined contribution plans.

Defined Benefit Plans

As explained in the chapter, there are many varieties of DB plans and the way the benefit is calculated. Typically, benefits payable will be a fraction of earnings called the accrual rate multiplied by years of employment. For example, the plan might pay 3 percent of the average of the best three years. As an example, let's use an employee who worked for the company for 20 years and whose best three years are $75,000, $80,000, and $85,000. The average is $80,000. Multiply $80,000 by 0.03, which is $2,400, and multiply that by 20 years of service. The basic pension the individual will receive is therefore $48,000 per year.

If you have a DB plan, you can obtain information about the specific benefit package from your employer's human resources department.

Defined Contribution Plans

DC plans hand to the employee the responsibility for investment and amounts that can be paid out. The plans typically pool money contributed by employees with the understanding that the collective amount of money will be invested by the plan sponsor. Employees who contribute often have the ability to select mutual funds from a menu provided by a designated manager that offers relatively low management fees in exchange for bulk business. There may be fixed income choices as well.

The best way to estimate DC plan pension benefits is to ask the sponsor, which will probably be the human resources department, for a statement of entitlements and then to make conservative assumptions about future contributions and rates of growth. Financial planners frequently assume that assets grow at 6 percent per year before any adjustment for inflation. If you assume 2.5 to 3 percent inflation for each year to retirement, you will be able to estimate future buying power.

Deferred Profit-Sharing Plans

The employer or sponsor runs these plans on a ledger basis or has an agent do so. The employer is in control, so check with the employer for your balance. DPSP proceeds must be paid not later than three months after employment ceases. Payments may be made over as much as a decade.

III. Individual Savings Plans

Individual savings plans, made up of Registered Retirement Savings Plans, Life Income Funds, Locked-In Retirement Accounts, and Locked-In Retirement Income Funds.

RRSPs

Contributions may run to the annuitant's 71st birthday or to the 71st birthday of a spouse or partner in a common-law relationship. Rates of increase of RRSP balances in accounts with heavy equity weighting cannot be predicted with accuracy. However, balances in high-quality fixed-income assets such as government bonds are predictable.

When converted to a Registered Retirement Income Fund, RRSP balances must be paid out with prescribed minimums per year. No maximums are imposed, however. See the table of RRIF minimum payouts in this chapter.

Locked-In Retirement Income Funds (LRIFs)

These are the same as RRIFs but with prescribed maximums. Check with the plan administrator for these limits.

Prescribed Registered Income Funds (PRIFs)

These are like RRIFs but with no maximum withdrawals or required purchase of an annuity. The PRIF, used in Saskatchewan and in a modified form in Manitoba, allows a person age 55 or older to do a one-time transfer of up to 50 percent of the value of the assets in a LIF or LRIF to a new PRIF.

IV. Annuities

Annuities are insurance-based pensions, made up of pensions funded by ordinary life policies and annuities. Each annuity contract is different. Check yours to determine annual payments.

V. Non-registered Assets

All other investments you hold outside an RRSP make up this category. Total the assets, decide what you need to take out each year to achieve your target retirement income, adjust for income tax deductions, and apply to total income.

VI. Fixed Assets

Real and Personal Property

A house, cars, boats, antiques, art, and so on can be sold and the cash applied to boost retirement income. Similarly, you can take a loan against a house, reamortize an existing mortgage on your house, or use a reverse mortgage to extract equity from a house. This can be a late-life move if you do not wish to bequeath your home to your children or others.

A Note on Inflation

Inflation is here to stay. Many economists predict it will run at 2 to 3 percent for the next few decades. When you are making your retirement plans, you cannot afford to ignore it. But there are ways to compensate for its effects.

The easiest way is just to take assumed rates of growth of income or assets and deduct 2 or 3 percent. So a predicted portfolio growth rate of 6 percent turns out to be 4 or 3 percent after inflation adjustment.

Defined benefit plans often have indexation built in, so the embedded risk is in assets that do not pace inflation.

Bonds, with returns of perhaps 4 to 5 percent before tax and inflation adjustment, offer little inflation protection. Preferred shares with fixed dividends likewise do it poorly. Common stocks that increase in value over time and that have rising dividends can do it relatively well. As do Real Return Bonds (RRBs), a special class of bonds that have a basic though low dividend, about 1.6 percent at time of writing, and then add an inflation adjustment. A 30-year RRB thus will have a return to maturity of 1.6% + 2.0% or 3.6%. That is low, but there is coverage for higher inflation rates if that should happen.

The younger the person, the more inflation protection required. The customary rule that says bonds should be the percentage of a portfolio equal to age allows for declining coverage for inflation. At age 80, you would have 80 percent bonds and 20 percent stocks. This is a rough guide, for the 20 percent might be high dividend stocks and allow for less bond investment, but the concept is clear: Always allow for some inflation fighters in a portfolio, if only because we cannot predict the future.

Chapter 7

Managing Retirement Assets

This chapter is about the creation and maintenance of retirement income through the direct management of assets. In the last two chapters, I discussed what amounts to passive income—that is, income that can flow today in recognition of previous work, of qualifying for Old Age Security, and of attaining the age required to cross the thresholds for company pensions and the Canada and Quebec Pension Plans. In this chapter, we'll see how income can be built up through active management. Management includes the decision to hire managers for your money, and these managers can be and indeed often are mutual funds. Alternatively, you may choose baskets of shares or bonds included in exchange-traded funds, which we noted in Chapter 2, or in index funds sold by mutual fund companies with usually below average fees. Like ETFs, index funds replicate various indices such as the S&P/TSX Total Return Index, a benchmark for all the stocks traded on the Toronto Stock Exchange.

Investing for retirement is full of schemes and short of truths. But there is one singular fact of investing that should guide every person moving toward retirement or already in it: *There is less time to make up for losses.* The older investor absolutely must not regard investing in stocks or other assets as he would a visit to a casino. The investment process for those over 55 or 60 has to be more cerebral, more disciplined, and certainly less impetuous than it is for younger people. After all, the older investor and even the investor in middle age may not have time or even the ability to boost employment income to recover losses in the stock market or in mutual funds. For the older investor, conservatism has to be the anchor of strategy. But with a difference. Inflation is the enemy of cash. Whatever asset mix the older investor may choose, it has to be something that, in the long run, can at least keep up with inflation after taxes on portfolio gains.

Time is on the side of the market, but that market has a shocking ability to turn gains into losses. For example, the Toronto Stock Exchange lost about half its value in the dot-com meltdown from 2000 to 2002. Anyone who wanted to get some cash out of technology stocks in that period had to accept that many of them were almost worthless and that raising any fixed amount of cash would require sale of vastly more stock than would have been necessary in 1999. In hindsight, it is easy to say that we should not have bought into companies with no earnings nor even sales, but the information "revolution" was underway and it was easy to get hooked. What is clear, however, is that those who did chase companies that boasted of their rates of burning up capital did so by abandoning their principles. After all, if there is a single concept that should guide investment, it is that destruction of capital is the very antithesis of building wealth.

The wise retiree should structure his or her financial assets for stability as well as growth. Diversification across asset classes like stocks, bonds, commodities, and real estate provides a form of stability. One class may rise as another falls. It is unlikely that all will tumble together. Indeed, in the Great Depression, even as stocks, commodities, and real estate prices fell, prices of government bonds soared. Another way to achieve stability is through use of stocks in portfolios blended with rising dividends, bonds, and fixed income mutual funds. Steady cash, after all, tends to smooth out the emotional booms and busts of the stock market.

Bank stocks, the shares of major non-bank financials like life insurance companies, and holding companies that own financial services businesses used to be more stable than shares of companies that dig up commodities like iron and gold. Yet in 2008, shares of banks and even life insurance companies were beaten down by investors' fears that financial institutions would have to write off alarming amounts of bad loans. Indeed, that is exactly what happened. In the second half of 2007 and in 2008, financial services were a drag on the market. Financial services mutual funds lost 31.4 percent for the 12 months ended June 30, 2008, compared to the 20.8 percent gain of natural resources equity funds in the same period. Clearly, diversification pays.

Conventional asset classes are stocks, bonds, and cash where cash is understood to include cash equivalents like Treasury bills (government bonds due in one year or less) and bankers acceptances (IOUs from chartered banks). That conventional classification is too narrow, however. The better classification would be stocks, bonds, cash and cash equivalents, real estate, commodities, life insurance, and annuities.

Most of the time, asset classes produce a ranking or risk-adjusted compound average annual returns as follows:

Asset Class	Return %/yr	Relative risk	Inflation compensation
Cash and equivalents	2%–4%	low	poor
Common stocks	8%	moderate	good over the long run
Investment grade bonds	5%	low	poor to moderate
Global real estate	2%	low	moderate
Commodities	variable	high	good over the long run
Life insurance	3%–8%	low	variable
Life annuities	3%–5%	low	poor

Investment Philosophies

There are half a dozen basic investment philosophies and scores of variations on these themes. Libraries of books discuss the theories, but for our purposes, we can review the leading concepts and put them into perspective.

The basic theories of buying stocks or bonds, property, commodities, and, for that matter, works of art and antiques are (1) value, (2) growth, (3) the hybrid style of growth at a reasonable price, and (4) momentum.

Value Investing

Value investing seeks to find the intrinsic worth of financial assets. For stocks, that may be the net worth of the company, the reliability of its dividends compared to bond interest, or even assets on the books that are not fully valued. Value investors like the fundamental concept of buying low and selling high. Some of the greatest investors, including Warren Buffet—head of Berkshire Hathaway, the holding company that has made him the wealthiest man in the United States as of 2008, surpassing even Microsoft's Bill Gates—have practised variations on buying low and selling high. Indeed, there is no other way to make money by trading assets. Every trading system ultimately is a buy-low, sell-high method in some form.

Value investors tend to look at measures of basic worth. There are many of them, including the customary ratios of share price to earnings per share, share price to free cash flow per share, share price to sales per share, and value of the parts of the business were they to be sold. Value investors are often classified into segments that range from relative-value stock pickers, who want shares that are cheap in relation to shares in similar businesses or markets; deep-value pickers, who want great deals; and bottom feeders, who are willing to pay bargain-basement prices for shares of what are often sick companies in the hope that they will recover. Value investors tend to focus on the price of stocks more than earnings trends in the customary valuation of price divided by earnings, usually written as p/e.

Value stock picking is a relatively low-risk way of investing. After all, the price of a stock selling at a low multiple of earnings has less far to fall than one that is priced at a high multiple of its earnings. But companies' stocks are often cheap for a reason. Their earnings may be unsteady or falling, they may be facing daunting competition, or they may be failing to execute their plans well. In 2008, the price multiples of auto parts makers in Canada tumbled in reaction to the rise of Chinese parts makers who turn out similar gear at a fraction of the North American cost.

The problem with all value stock picking is that the practitioners have to believe that the stocks they find, no matter how ignored or beaten up, will eventually become popular. If those stocks remain market pariahs and stay in what the market calls a value trap, then shares may not rise to reflect their value. The risks of the value trap are greatest for tiny companies that are not monitored by investment analysts. The risks are lowest for large caps that are always in view and followed by many analysts. But value traps do exist and the reason that value fund managers can co-exist without pumping up the prices of many wallflower stocks is, quite simply, that there are so many stocks nobody really cares about. Thus value investing ultimately rests on a tautology—there are good stocks few see and fewer care about and those stocks will remain hidden from many or most investors unless they go out and do their own digging. For those that do—and do it well—the rewards can be quite substantial.

Growth Investing

Growth investing worries less about the price you pay for an asset than the rate of growth of the market price of the asset. Growth investors in the stock market focus on the rate of rise of earnings per share or cash flow per share. Growth investing takes a good deal of attention to follow changing estimates of corporate earnings. If growth investors wind up paying too much for stocks, as they did in the dot-com era when it was acceptable in some circles to pay 100 to 200 times annual estimated earnings per share, they can lose very badly in corrections. By contrast, value investors tended not to buy into the dot-com frenzy, for companies with hugely inflated multiples of their earnings and companies with high share prices in spite of having no earnings and even no revenues were not on the value investors' screens.

Growth investors have at least as many talismans of worth as value investors. Analysts and portfolio managers who practise the art of finding terrific companies destined to become even more terrific look for upgrades by analysts, positive earnings surprises, rapid increases in expected future earnings, and insights into the next great thing. The trick in this school of investing is to get in early and to be well informed. It is a demanding craft. Growth investors tend to focus on the "e" part of the p/e valuation measure.

Growth investors have to face the reality that no company can maintain a high growth rate forever. The principle that exceptional rates of growth of earnings will eventually fall to the level of those of competing companies in the same industries is an extension of the statistical principle of mean reversion. Over time, companies that grow very large will find their rates of growth trending down toward market averages. The highest-growth-rate companies have average rates of growth of earnings 20 percentage points higher than the average growth rate for the lowest-earnings-growth companies in the year during which results are screened. Five years later, the differences converge to close to zero.[1]

Growth at a Reasonable Price

Growth at a reasonable price, sometimes called GARP for short, is a hybrid that seeks to measure the ratio of price to earnings (p/e) per share divided by estimated growth (g) of earnings per share. This PEG ratio can be used to find relative bargains. Thus a stock with a 20 p/e ratio and a 25 percent average annual rate of growth of earnings is a relative bargain for the p/e ratio is less than the g growth rate of profits. Stock with PEG ratios under 1 therefore qualify as good buys, those with higher PEG ratios up to 1.5 or so may be relatively good buys, and those with high PEG ratios over 2 or 3 or more, depending on the analyst, will not appeal to GARP investors.

In a study concluded in 1998, Morgan Stanley found that a strategy of buying stocks with low PEG ratios yielded returns that were significantly higher than returns of the benchmark Standard & Poor's 500 Composite. The 100 stocks with the lowest PEG ratios earned annual returns of 18.7 percent in the period from 1986 to 1998 compared to the benchmark average annual return of 16.8 percent. But investing by PEG ratios is a risky business on its own, for the process of comparison tends to discount or even ignore the risk of unsteady earnings. A portfolio of stocks with the lowest PEG ratios will therefore tend to include a large number of high-risk stocks.[2] After all, a company whose earnings vary from gaining 100 percent one year and losing 50 percent the next has no net growth at all. In dollar terms over two years, it will rise from, say, $8 to $16 in year 1, then lose $8 in year 2. In actual dollars, it has gained nothing at all over two years. On a percentage basis, however, it is up an average of 100%–50% = 50%/2 or 25% per year. Beware false profits.

In the end, GARP stocks may just be traders rather than keepers, that is, stocks that fall into a range of valuation that a GARP stock picker finds acceptable that are then sold when the stock rises out of the range of acceptability of the GARP formula. GARP is, therefore, a sort of safety screen against paying too much for growth stocks, but it is a screen with a cost in potentially high portfolio turnover and related transactions costs.

Momentum Investing

Momentum investing takes several forms. There are earnings momentum investors who say, with some statistical justification, that companies that show strong earnings growth are likely to continue that trend in successive periods. The idea of a continuing trend extends to the most precarious of all theories, price momentum, which asserts that a stock on the way up will continue its journey. There is some evidence that supports the idea that a momentum-based stock-picking strategy can outperform a broad market index, but the concept of momentum investing tends to require very high levels of portfolio management. It tends to lead to high portfolio turnover and, in non-tax deferred accounts such as RRSPs, to frequent taxation of gains. It is, moreover, the antithesis of buy-and-hold investing. The process of momentum investing can work in the right hands, but it is a precarious way to make a living.

Cynics say that stocks are not value or growth or GARP or momentum, that they are just in stages on a merry-go-round. Thus small companies may be ignored. When they get some cash flow and earnings, they may be selling at lower multiples of sales or cash flow than companies with established profits. At this stage, these newcomers are value stocks. The companies continue to thrive and get their growth rates up. Now the stocks become GARP picks. When the valuations rise too far above what GARP investors are willing to pay, they become unabashed growth stocks. If they are really hot, they become momentum stocks. And if the companies do not deliver expected performance, they are sold off and can become value stocks once more. Research In Motion, RIM for short, the maker of the BlackBerry wireless communication device, has wound up with one of the largest market caps in Canada on the basis of moves from value to growth to momentum. Where RIM may go is anyone's guess, but it is also a sure thing that it cannot rise forever. Eventually, earnings stabilize. Growth subsides and the high-price multiple that the stock once attained slips.

QUESTION: How do value investing, growth investing, and GARP investing differ?

ANSWER: Value investors concentrate on price and seek to buy shares at low prices (p) in terms of earnings (e). Growth investors concentrate on growth and worry less about the prices they pay. GARP investors put p and e together to get a measure of what they have to pay for growth.

Are Asset Prices Really Predictable?

The concept of trend continuity has some value in stock analysis, but there is another school of investing that holds that all stock price movements are random. Burton G. Malkiel, a Princeton University economist, popularized the idea that stock prices could not be predicted in his 1973 bestseller, *A Random Walk Down Wall Street*. The concept of unpredictability of stock prices has to be balanced with the evidence that at least some managers manage to beat market averages for extended periods. In Canada, numerous mutual funds and pension funds managed by companies like McLean Budden Limited, Dynamic Funds, and Sceptre Investment Counsel Ltd. have outperformed Canadian and U.S. markets for extended periods.

The reasons that professional managers can beat markets and the average investor over periods of a few years is simple: They know more. They get invited to lunch with company presidents, have the privilege of quizzing chief financial officers, have squads of analysts specialized in industries and even in single companies, and are focused on stock picking—their main job. In a survey of

results of Bay Street versus Main Street, the *Globe and Mail* found
that in 2007, professional fund managers' 20 top stocks generated
returns of 19.2 percent compared to returns of just 7.9 percent
generated by the 20 top stocks held by retail investors. The data for
the survey comes from the Globe's own websites, but it is indica-
tive of the ability of professionals to beat amateurs.[3]

No truth is forever. Bill Miller, the manager of the US$17.3-
billion Legg Mason Value Trust, beat the S&P 500 Composite for
15 straight years through 2005, a record for mutual fund
managers. But for the two consecutive years ended December 31,
2007, he trailed his benchmark index. In 2006, he lagged behind
99 percent of similar equity funds with a modest 6 percent gain. In
2007, he ranked in the bottom 2 percent of peers. They averaged
a 6.2 percent return. The causes—holding losing stocks. The Value
Trust held both Citigroup, which fell 47 percent in 2007, and Sears
Holdings Corp., which fell 39 percent in the same period.[4] Bad
picks, bad timing, or even bad luck can happen to even the most
gifted managers.

How to handle money appears to come down to a single
decision made from two choices: (1) try to beat the market or
(2) join the market and go for a ride. Value investing, growth
investing, and momentum investing are expressions of the belief
that you can find winning stocks and therefore beat the market.
Alternatively, you can decide to do the very opposite of asset selection—give up and let the market do as it will. This school of
thought leads quite directly to index investing, the idea that it is
very hard to beat markets over the long run and that the investor's
best shot at prosperity lies in nothing more than betting on major
indices like the S&P 500 Composite.

Fees and Performance

Funds that concentrate on investment grade bonds are particularly exposed to economic trends. In bond investing, when interest rates appear to be rising rapidly, existing bonds decline in price. That's because investors will be reluctant to pay the present price for an interest coupon that will seem modest in a few months. Existing bonds will drop in price. The wise course will be stay in cash or Treasury bills. Good bond fund managers can do that, but bond index funds with average terms to maturity will see their values plummet. There is wisdom and value to be had in professionally managed portfolios. The trick is to find the winners nimble enough to go with the currents of rising markets and assets and go against the rough waters of falling markets and declining assets

Funds and Costs

Picking mutual funds is a skill unto itself. It is enough to suggest that you diversify, select funds for long-term performance, and keep fees in view. There are high-fee funds with poor performance and low-fee funds with excellent performance. The average management fee for Canadian stock funds is 2.4 percent. If you hold the fund for 20 years, you will pay 48 percent of your initial contribution to the manager. If the fund lags the market or just fails to grow with the market, you will lose. Never lose sight of fees.

A few rules for judging a fund by its fee:

1. The narrower the asset class, the less management skill matters. Canadian government bonds are a narrow asset class. Managers tend to be able to add little to returns. Any fee over

1 percent in a class in which returns tend to vary from 4 to 5 percent per year (and this is in good years) is excessive.

2. The wider the asset class, the more a manager can do to add value. Global stocks are difficult for individuals to trade. The research requirements are prodigious, and the complexities of currencies and withholding taxes are daunting. You can leave this sort of asset class to a manager or management company with a proven record. Potential gains in the double digits allow for higher management fees of perhaps 2 to 3 percent. But the investor must remain vigilant to ensure that performance and fees stay in balance.

3. Funds with high turnovers tend to be short-term wonders. Trading rates and returns are inversely related. Turnover generates taxable events and the taxes, which are paid out of fund assets, do nothing for the investor's wealth. On the other hand, funds with consistent philosophies or disciplines that the managers follow conscientiously are worth considering.

4. Mutual funds are always profitable for those who run them and for salespeople. They are not necessarily profitable for their investors. Mutual fund advice books used to be abundant. Within the last few years, publishers have deferred to data sources like http://www.globefund.com. Learn the territory and understand the bottom-line truth of fund investing: There are no portfolios that are permanent winners and few that are permanent losers. Therefore seek out funds that appear to have relatively steady, above-average performance and reasonable fees. Seeking out the funds that dance on the high wire of performance can lead to disasters. Above all, ensure that the funds you consider offer fee-efficient performance. The higher the fee, the more you should expect and receive.

Index Investing

Over periods of decades, fees create headwinds for managed funds. Rather than pay average managed equity fund fees of say, 2.4 percent per year, you can buy units in an index fund packaged and sold as an exchange-traded fund that may have management fees of 15 or 20 basis points (a basis point is 1/100th of 1 percent). Over 20 years, the low-fee fund will then generate fees of 4 percent. The difference between that fee and a 48 percent fee, which—ignoring a little compounding—is the charge for 20 years of 2.4 percent per year fees, is massive. It is no wonder that index investing has become very popular in the last few decades. Today, many individual investors are index investors. They imitate large pension funds, which often commit parts of their portfolios to index replication.

Index investing became popular in the 1970s as mathematical analysis of portfolio manager performance became widely used by insurance companies and pension funds. Returns by money managers have lagged major indices for several decades, and market timing, which is the practice of making what appear to be wise buy and sell decisions at trend turning points, has not appeared to work well. The market has seemed to beat many or even most of the best minds on Wall and Bay streets. No wonder the investment community has come to doubt the wisdom of paying hefty fees for the privilege of lagging the very benchmarks on which performance is judged.

Index investing, which ignores selection of specific stocks or bonds in favour of buying whole sectors or markets, would seem to be idiot proof, but it is not. For better or worse, an index fund is always in a position to benefit from its market on the way up or to suffer from it when it is headed down. On the other hand, good managers can dodge bullets by avoiding holding what they think are stocks on the way down and adding weight to those they think will rise.

Over time, however, the high cumulative costs of managed funds tend to outweigh the benefits of skilful management. Thus the odds of an index fund beating a managed fund rise over time. The bigger the gap, the more brilliant and sustained the performance of the managed fund has to be to beat the low-fee index fund. And in some cases, there is so little for a manager to do with an asset mix that the odds lie mostly with the indexed portfolio.

QUESTION: Why do index funds have a long-term advantage over managed mutual funds?

ANSWER: They have fees a small fraction of those of the managed funds. A difference of a few percent on fees can make a huge difference in returns after 10 or 20 years.

Index Funds

The virtues of index investing—low fees and a good chance of beating the pants off most managed funds—have propelled index investing into prominence. Today, you can buy index-based exchange-traded funds that hold so-called ethical stocks, growth stocks, value stocks, global stocks with large or small capitalizations, stocks subject to maximum levels or caps in funds, European pharmaceutical stocks, funds that track the Morgan Stanley Real Estate Investment Trust Index, Pacific Rim stocks, bond and stock mixes, and bonds of specified terms from short to long. Canadian investors can buy indexes that hedge exposure to currencies to prevent a rise in the loonie from cutting into underlying asset returns. Indeed, by creating a portfolio of index funds, you can eliminate all worries about buying specific companies or bonds. The only decision that the investor need make is about sector allocations and fees charged by index funds.

With index funds, investors can arguably be said to be insulated from the dangerous hype that surrounds successful managed funds. When a mutual fund has a banner year, investors tend to flood it with money. The manager may not be able to invest it as well as he did when the fund began its year of ascent, perhaps in a time when stock or bond prices were lower. Propelled by a rising market and some good management or even just risky plunges into assets in favour, the fund has a good year. Then money cascades in. But the market may change. The winning stocks of last year may be overpriced this year. Buying at the top, as successful funds are often obliged to do if they have mandates to stay fully invested, becomes a recipe for a collapse. It happens all too often.

The index fund rises and falls with the market, but it is immune from managed fund hype. If the world comes knocking at your stock's door and if the fund is fairly narrowly defined, both the index and the managed fund will be vulnerable to a correction of the shares of any firm in the sector. But in a widely based fund such as the Morgan Stanley Capital International Index, which tracks global enterprise in many countries around the world, including Canada, difficulties in any one firm or even any one country are unlikely to harm the fund's total performance.

Exchange-traded funds tend to have no sales fees apart from market sales commissions. Those charges can be very small if you use an online discount broker. Index funds are also tax-efficient in that they do not trade or change their holdings very much. Thus you can buy and sell them just as you would ordinary shares. The investor can be aware of capital gains and losses that an index fund trade may create but should not make tax minimization the only important variable.

To get even further from market forces, you can use trading strategies that average out costs. Through cost averaging, you can buy 100 shares every month on, say, the 15th of the month or the business day closest to it, and you wind up ignoring market trends. Or you can use value averaging by setting a goal of buying the same 100 units, but reducing the order to 50 units if the index fund is up by 5 percent over the last month's closing fund price or adding 50 units if the fund is 5 percent below the last month's closing fund price. Finally, you can be an absolutely contrarian investor by selling half or all the index funds in a portfolio that have produced the largest gains in a single year and adding to the holding with the index funds that have produced the lowest performance in the year. You can also use a larger roster of index funds and do the very same thing. Statistical measures show that buying losers and selling winners produces much higher returns than the strategy, often followed by passive investors, of buying the winners and selling the losers.[5]

Bonds

The value of owning bonds is that they tend to rise in price when stocks are falling. That makes them a form of insurance for a portfolio. Under conditions of high inflation, both bonds and stocks can suffer, but double-digit inflation as it existed in the 1970s is not in sight.

It is important to pick the right bonds. Many retirees would like to hold Government of Canada bonds, which have no credit problems. One government bond is pretty much like another, though each bond's responsiveness to interest rate changes will be different. There is room for variation, for a manager could go 100 percent to 30-year bonds if he were sure that a depression was about to break out and interest rates were going to tumble, thus raising the value of fixed coupons. Or he could go 100 percent to cash or Treasury bills if he were sure that interest rates were about to soar and make the value of existing bonds with their fixed coupons plummet. Some bond funds mix in corporate bonds. Judicious use of corporate bonds can add to bond portfolio returns.

In practice, most bond fund managers stick rather closely to their own bond benchmarks. If the index is 60 percent government bonds and 40 percent corporates and has a duration (sensitivity to changes in interest rates) of, say, 6.7 years (the way this sensitivity is measured), chances are that bond fund managers will be close to it. For anyone who wants the benefits of being able to buy and sell bonds with low spreads between the wholesale price that the investment dealer pays and the retail price that the investor pays, a bond fund makes sense. There is a tradeoff of a sort between efficient bond investing and the high fees most managed bond funds charge. Still, real bonds revert to cash, something no bond fund ever does.

Segregated Funds

There is an alternative to buying index funds or trying to time returns by trading. Segregated funds, which are ordinary mutual funds wrapped into a kind of insurance policy, provide a guarantee that, in exchange for a surcharge, the investor will get back not less than 80 percent or 100 percent of the initial contribution, usually after 10 years. Segregated funds, bought well in advance of a personal bankruptcy, offer broad though not total protection from creditor claims as well. Finally, seg funds have a life insurance guarantee that, if the owner dies within the 10-year period, the plans will pay beneficiaries the greater of market value of assets or initial cost. These benefits are of substantial value as portfolio insurance.[6]

The problem with segregated funds arises with their costs. If the annual asset insurance surcharge is, say, three-fourths of 1 percent, then after 10 years, the investor will have paid 7.5 percent for the guarantee. But statistics show that funds over 10 years have odds of at least covering their initial price or net asset value at purchase 19 out of 20 times. That's a 5 percent chance of loss. So, in this example, you pay 7.5 percent to insure a 5 percent loss risk. Creditor protection is worth something and, because seg funds are considered a life insurance product, they can be shepherded to named heirs without probate. That's worth something too. But the basic proposition is that there can be no loss. However, there is no coverage for inflation. What's more, anyone can create equivalent seg fund cost recovery by buying a stripped 10-year government bond sold at a discount by investment dealers that handle stocks and bonds, investing the difference in any asset at all, and, in 10 years, the worst possible outcome is total recovery of the initial price of the strip at maturity. Thus to insure a $100,000 portfolio, buy a strip at, say, $65,000, invest the balance of $35,000 in stocks, and wait. You cannot come out with less than $100,000 and if the stock market has been good, you could have an average return of, say, 7 percent a year or 97 percent on the stocks on a compounded basis. Just holding cash idle would provide a return of $100,000 plus $35,000.

We should not rush to dismiss all seg funds, however. Someone who bought a high-tech fund in 1998 with a seg fund guarantee would be smiling in 2008. Even after a decade of recovery, tech funds that imploded in 2000–2002 would have left their owners with an average annual compound loss of 0.5 percent per year. Tech funds with no seg fund protection would be worth just 61 percent of the original investment for the 10 years ended June 30, 2008. Clearly, the more volatile a mutual fund category, the more a seg fund return of principal guarantee is worth. However, like consistent investment purchases on a fixed sum per month basis, seg funds take timing issues out of the equation. Thus to insure or not is also, like other investment issues, complicated by what can be called the luck of the draw.

Umbrella Plans

Investment planning is easy in theory. You assume a rate of return, design a portfolio to fund expenses in retirement, and everything should work out well. Unfortunately, the world does not obey theories. Too often, markets devastate well-laid plans.

Manulife and several other money managers have come up with schemes that level out income in spite of market swings. The concept responds to a real problem: If in the decade before you convert an RRSP to a RRIF or an annuity, the market plunges and fails to recover, then the sum available for conversion may be drastically reduced.

The people most at risk are those with defined contribution pension plans, RRSPs, and even non-registered investments. Manulife's Income Plus (IP) plan is a defence against wealth erosion by market decline. The IP plan offers a guaranteed minimum withdrawal benefit in a kind of hybrid of an annuity that offers a fixed income for life and a segregated mutual fund that puts a floor under portfolio losses.[7]

Income Plus provides an annual withdrawal of 5 percent of the fund value. The amounts that can be withdrawn are variable, but at 5 percent the plan can produce payments for the life of the person for whom the plan is purchased. This sounds like a cousin to an annuity, but it is actually both more and less than that. Like a stock portfolio, the Income Plus concept allows for portfolio gains. Conventional annuity contracts don't do that. Balances can be reset at the end of every third year, locking in market gains. If the investor elects to skip a 5 percent withdrawal for a year, a corresponding bonus is added to what Manulife calls "the guaranteed withdrawal balance," which is the base for subsequent payments. And there is an option that allows the IP plan to function like an annuity that provides income for life. For more information, see http://www.manulifeincomeplus.ca.

The Income Plus package of guarantees bears management fees up to 3.5 percent, which is at the high end of mutual fund charges. Critics say that it's no more than an expensive way to guarantee income.[8] They note that you could achieve much the same thing at a lower cost with a ladder of guaranteed income certificates.

An investment product not much more than a year old offers immediate or deferred income with a promise to return all monies invested and something that annuities cannot provide—participation in their upside sectors of the stock and bond markets. Created and sold by Dynamic Funds as "Retirement Edge Income Portfolios," they use several value and growth funds and domestic and foreign assets including bonds and have the added benefit that distributions are considered returns of capital. There is a risk of a large tax bite on interest paid when deferred payment contracts terminate. But there is a way out of this bind. If the investor sells a few months or weeks before maturity, the sale price of Retirement Edge units, which are technically deposits at a chartered bank in excess of the adjusted cost base, should be taxed as capital gains. If held to maturity, all returns above original capital will be taxed at full value as interest.[9]

Retirement Edge portfolios raise bond allocations and lower income levels as the investor grows older. The portfolios come in three flavours—current pay notes that offer annual income of 6.6 percent of net amount invested with annual inflation adjustments. There are also two deferred income versions: a 5-year note with a 12-year term with an 8.25 percent annual payout of amount invested with distributions beginning in year 6 after purchase and deferred 10-year notes with 9.9 percent annual payouts beginning in year 11 after purchase and running for 10 years. Both the 5- and 10-year notes can be carried another 5 years with no distributions should the investor wish to postpone taxation. Each variation has unlimited upside potential and a downside that is expressed as a minimum payout: 5 percent per year minimum gain in income for the 5-year note for a 25 percent total gain and 50 percent growth for the 10-year version. The value of this product is that it guarantees to return every penny put into the fund, to add at least defined gains. As well, Retirement Edge provides potential tax deferral. The rates of return are those in effect in mid-2008 and may change with market conditions.[10]

Real Estate

We are all investors in property. Either we own houses outright with no obligations to lenders, own property with a mortgage, or rent. Even renters are property "owners" in an economic sense, for they pay for the shelter they occupy. The difference, of course, is that in a legal sense, renters have no direct exposure to capital gains or losses on property.

A home of one's own differs from a speculative investment in property. A house or condo provides shelter, which is something that no stock or bond or mutual fund can do. Even if house prices decline, the home continues to be a fundamental investment.

Homes are far from certain to provide capital gains. In the last decade, home prices around the world have soared. But in the housing price crisis that began in 2007 with the collapse of the market for poor-quality mortgages in the United States, once-impregnable home prices have tumbled. The widely used S&P/Case-Shiller Home Prices Index shows that U.S. home prices dropped 14.1 percent in the 12 months ended March 31, 2008, compared to the same period a year earlier. That was the largest drop in the 20-year span of the index. Among the most affected cities were Las Vegas, which recorded a 25.9 percent drop, and Miami, which produced a 24.6 percent drop in the 12 months ended March 31, 2007. Canada has a much sounder mortgage market and, as a result, Canadian house prices were relatively stable during the credit crisis of 2007 to 2008. Yet the dramatic drop in American prices shows how much and how suddenly a sure thing can turn to a disaster.

Property prices are therefore no different than those of other assets: They rise and fall with other markets. Scarcity of land and economic conditions influence prices, of course. But there is one other determinant unique to residential property—affordability.

If home prices rise far above the ability of people to pay for shelter, there will be a correction. That, in a sense, is happening as I write this chapter. The U.S. residential home market has imploded. People unable to afford increased payments on mortgages that had deferred interest arrangements have been fleeing their properties or, more tragically, losing their homes to lenders. We do not have to go into the details of the U.S. subprime disaster, save to note that the principle that affordability brings house prices back to earth has not lost its logic or its force. Thus in Canada, prices have declined in Ontario, stabilized in parts of British Columbia, and will surely settle down in the Alberta oil patch. After all, if nobody can afford to buy a house or to purchase one from a speculative investor, there has to be a price retreat. The moral of this is quite simple: Don't buy into what you cannot afford and don't buy into a runaway real estate market price trend. Nothing lasts forever.

Many homeowners view their properties as fixed assets. That's true in the sense that a well-maintained house or a condo in a well-run development will last a long time and perhaps hold its value or even grow in value. But there is an alternative way of looking at a house. That's to see it as a stage for one part of life and as a stepping stone to another. Thus a person or couple with a large home can use it to raise children and even to provide accommodation for visiting grandchildren. The house can provide room for someone who may give personal care to an elderly person. But at some time the house may become more than you need. Then it can be sold or "rightsized" with a capital gain taken and a smaller, less expensive house purchased. The second home could also be a rental accommodation. The capital gain from the sale of a principal residence is not subject to Canadian income taxation, so the sale may generate a very large boost to the capital base of the person moving into smaller quarters.

The alternative to downsizing a home is to reduce your personal use of it. You may decide to convert part of your house to an income property. Renting out a room or an apartment does that. There are tax implications for this conversion. As well, if the person renting out the home decides to take depreciation on the house in order to reduce taxable income, the part of the house that is depreciated will no longer be eligible for full exemption from capital gains taxes. When you are getting close to the time when you want to sell the house, it is unwise to impair the capital gains exemption.

There are other ways to invest in real estate. You can buy a Real Estate Investment Trust or REIT. Many of these investments have performed well. You can choose specialized funds that buy global properties, hotels, shopping centres, and other well-defined types of property. They are run by managers who usually have experience in real estate investment. The funds provide diversification and allow for small or frequent redemptions, something that cannot be done if you have diversified into one or even a few rental or speculative investments.

Reverse Mortgages

The Canadian Home Income Plan, often called CHIP, has popularized the idea of selling a future interest in your home in exchange for present income. The system seems straightforward. You, the homeowner, borrow against your property. You get a cash payment as a lump sum and make no periodic repayments. At death or at some time in future, you repay the loan. Because interest and principal have been deferred, the debt has compounded. Repayment tends to be very costly, but the concept appeals to older people who want to live in their homes and do not want to downsize or move to rental housing. It has been reported that 12 percent of Canadian senior citizens use their homes as a source of retirement income.[11] Statistics Canada has reported that senior citizens have 77 percent of their net worth in their homes.[12] Tapping it seems to make sense.

The idea of the reverse mortgage is not wrong. It is just a way of reamortizing a home and deferring repayment. The money received can be spent or used to buy an annuity, thus converting the capital of the home into income. If the home appreciates, then the repayment may seem easier. But the future interest of the owner is at stake. If a person or a couple wants to include the house in an estate for children or charity, then there will be much less to pass on unless the real estate market is bullish enough to rescue the value of the home.

Let's look at a typical deal with a house appraised at $600,000. Based on that value, the owners could qualify for a $221,500 loan. CHIP lends conservatively, that is, only an amount that, even with interest, they can recapture at sale. If the loan rate is 9 percent, the borrower would owe $796,600 after 15 years. If the home appreciates by 6 percent per year, it would be worth $1.4 million after 15 years, leaving $603,400 in net equity. CHIP and a competitor, Seniors Money Ltd., claim that no one can ever owe more than the value of the house. Yet if the borrower lives long enough, that is precisely what could happen. The initial low loan-to-value ratios of the reverse mortgage companies make this outcome unlikely but certainly not impossible.[13]

The CHIP and Seniors Money plans are similar, but there are significant differences. CHIP sets its interest rate at prime plus 2 percent. Seniors Money sets its rate at prime plus 1.25 percent. It seems that Seniors Money would be less costly, but note that CHIP compounds its interest rates semi-annually and offers some discounts on its interest rates. Seniors Money interest due compounds monthly and does not have discounts.[14]

A more conservative way of getting money out of a house is just to remortgage it. Take the money, make periodic interest and principal payments, obtain mortgage life insurance if it is available from an independent insurance agent (not from the lender—prices tend to be high at banks and other lenders), and preserve the value of the estate. This is, of course, more easily said than done. Two-thirds of Canadians now in middle age will have trouble making ends meet when they retire, according to a University of Waterloo study released June 14, 2007.[15] In the end, the reverse mortgage and its cheaper alternative, remortgaging through a conventional financial institution, are desperate measures that address what amounts to a lack of planning or perhaps unsuccessful planning for retirement, says Derek Moran, a financial planner in Kelowna, B.C. "The costs are high in relation to the benefits," he explains. The difference between a reverse mortgage and conventional mortgage is repayment. A reverse mortgage requires no payments until death or sale of the house, then the piper has to be paid. A conventional mortgage is a pay-as-you-go arrangement without compounding interest for interest that has not been paid. Either way, the process can be fairly painless if the home increases in value. If the home should fall in value, as houses and condos have in the subprime disaster in the United States, it is possible to wind up owing more than a home is worth.

Monetizing Other Assets

Remortgaging a home by creating or extending a mortgage for a number of years is a process of converting capital to income. The process is not unique to housing, for it can be done with any capital asset. It has become common with homes because banks have traditionally liked to lend against fixed assets.

The same process of converting capital to income can be done with other assets. Sell a valuable collection of coins or a prized antique car and, provided that there has been appreciation and that you have been able to capture it in the sale, you are taking capital and turning it into cash that can be spent.

The principle extends to human capital. The student who studies to enter a profession is in a position to turn the capital value of education into income. Likewise, the person with a profession who allows it to lapse through lack of practice or failure to keep up with professional education in his or her field is destroying human capital. Of course, if the professional or tradesman or office worker goes back to work and puts experience to work, then the process of extracting income from capital is at work again.

That is precisely the principle at play in the plans of a significant minority of baby boomers who refuse to let their professional accomplishments go to waste. A survey of 304 baby boomers by polling firm Ipsos Reid for the Bank of Montreal done in early October 2007 showed that 15 percent of baby boomers in the age range of 45 to 60 who retired early to start their own businesses said that they plan to work "until they die." One in five of the people polled said he or she expects to run a businesses for more than a decade while 38 percent said they would work for six to ten years. Only 16 percent said they would work for less than five years. Those polled explained their intent to work as personal fulfillment, a wish to be occupied, or a need for money.[16] One can add that the longer the period of retirement or the less well indexed a pension is, the more likely it is that boredom or the need for supplementary income will push retirees back into the labour force or push them to sell assets for cash.

Viatical Settlements

Life insurance policies can be cash cows for the living as well as for the dead. When policy holders are very ill and desperately in need of cash, they may be able to sell the death benefit of their insurance to third parties. These "viatical settlements" are controversial, but they offer what amounts to a life jacket to those who are terminally ill and urgently in need of cash.

In a typical viatical settlement, a company that acts as a broker between the very ill insured person and the potential investor will offer to buy the life insurance policy for a lump sum that is a fraction of the total future death benefit. The owner of the policy, the viator, can then receive money before his or her death. The broker has an asset that it can resell to a third party for a profit. The viator might get 60 percent of the death benefit if the insured is expected to live less than two years and 80 percent if death is expected in less than six months. When death does occur, the investor who bought the policy receives the total death benefit.

In the United States, viatical settlements began to be arranged when AIDS deaths were rising in the gay community in the late 1980s. In that context, viatical settlements made sense, for gay men often did not have children that their life insurance might have supported after their deaths. The downside of the viatical settlements industry was the booming—and highly profitable—brokerage industry that grew up to connect the terminally ill with investors.

It is a business with ethical issues. The buyer of another person's life insurance policy has a financial interest in that person's death. The sooner it happens, the better off the investor is. The money the investor pays will vary with estimates of the ill person's condition and interest rates. For the investor, purchase of another person's life insurance benefits is a difficult to quantify risk at a cost that grows more uncertain as the time to death lengthens. In the usual viatical settlement, the investor will have to take over the premium payments. Thus the cost of the investment is unknown.

From the point of view of the seller of benefits, relinquishing benefits to a third party is equally risky. But need can trump risk, and so this curious branch of the insurance market continues to exist. There have been attempts to regulate the viatical industry, but the fundamental appeal of receiving benefits before death continues to support the concept. As well, in the United States, the industry that provides viatical settlements has moved beyond AIDS and other terminal illnesses to a focus on senior citizens.[17]

Viatical settlements remain relatively rare in Canada, but, as in the United States, there is a core issue of exploitation of the sick or elderly. The amount paid by the investor who takes over a life insurance policy should be less than the death benefit. The size of the discounts in the 1980s and the 1990s in the United States made some critics of the viatical settlements industry call it ghoulish.[18]

In Canada, life insurance carriers have opposed viatical settlements. They take the view that benefits that can be paid when life expectancy is less than two years provide assistance equivalent to viatical settlements.

According to the Canadian Life and Health Insurance Association, a Toronto-based industry group, the policy holder can obtain advanced death benefits by speaking with the insurance carrier and providing evidence of terminal illness. The carrier can then accelerate part of the death benefit of the policy. The amount paid would be deducted from the amount eventually paid to named beneficiaries or to the estate of the deceased policy holder, according to Frank Zinatelli, vice-president for legal services and associate general counsel at the CLHIA. "The payouts for persons who are terminally ill can be in the vicinity of 50 percent of the policy death benefit," he explained.

As well, legislative prohibitions on trafficking in life insurance policies has inhibited the growth of the viatical settlement industry in Canada. There remain good reasons for viatical settlements to grow in Canada, in spite of the potential for abuse of the sick and the elderly. For their part, insurance companies dislike viatical settlements because of the potential for fraud they present, Zinatelli said. In the United States, people have falsified medical records, obtained life insurance, and then sold policies for viatical settlements. This results in what amounts to a premature claim of benefits.[19] For now, in Canada, law and custom make it hard to obtain viatical settlements. The four provinces that allow viatical settlements, Zinatelli says, are Saskatchewan, New Brunswick, Quebec, and Nova Scotia. Only these provinces have no legislative prohibitions on viatical settlements. Even in a province that permits viatical settlements, if one can find a person to buy a life insurance policy, the transaction would have to be checked by a lawyer to ensure that it does not offend anti-trafficking laws. And as a financial matter, the transaction would have to be examined by an actuary for fairness to both sides. As well, the payment from a viatical provider may be considered taxable income, unlike payment from an insurance policy, which would be exempt to a named beneficiary under the Income Tax Act.

Chapter Summary

Asset management is really a form of risk control. As you grow older, the value of risk reduction becomes apparent. The reason— there is less time to make up for losses if an investment sours. One cannot predict how any stock or even any sector may perform in a certain time period, so diversification among many stocks, sectors, and asset types is essential. A well-diversified portfolio may have stocks, bonds, and perhaps some real estate. As well, the investor has to be aware of tax issues that affect cash flow.

Chapter 7 Appendix

Tax Matters

Tax management is vital for a financially successful retirement. Seniors have the benefit of certain tax breaks not available to younger people, but the benefits are frequently dependent on income. Thus in planning for breaks, it is vital to manage your tax exposure. Where there are tax credits available for seniors, it makes sense to check your qualifications for them. Some credits are refundable, that is, payable in cash. You may be tempted to get around the system by failing to report income in order to qualify for these credits. This is not a wise course. Informed compliance is the best course. To that end, this appendix offers some tips.

The OAS Clawback

The most obvious tax on benefits is the Old Age Security clawback, which hits taxpayers whose net income exceeds more than $64,718 in 2008. It takes back 15 percent of the amount by which net income exceeds the threshold. At an income level of $105,000, Old Age Security benefits are fully taken back.

The clawback tax on Old Age Security payments is deducted from monthly benefits cheques or direct deposits to accounts at financial services institutions. The amount withheld is based on net income in the prior two years.

It is possible to reduce the clawback's effects. That can be done by income averaging, by deferring recognition of income or capital gains, or by accelerating tax losses. This should be done in compliance with the Income Tax Act and may require advice from a tax professional. You should apply for OAS benefits six to twelve months before your 65th birthday.

Age Credit

People over age 65 by the end of the year for which an individual tax return is filed receive an additional federal tax credit. The amount for 2007 was $802. The credit is linked to income and is reduced by 15 percent of net income over $30,936. Therefore the credit is eliminated when net income exceeds $65,449. The spouse's net income does not affect the calculation.

Quebec provides a 20 percent non-refundable tax credit similar to the federal age credit for those 65 and older and for pension income. The Quebec age credit is worth up to $440 and the Quebec pension credit is worth as much as $300. The amounts available for claims for these two credits and for the Quebec living-alone credit are added and then reduced by 15 percent of Quebec family net income in excess of $29,290.

Pension Income Credit

Seniors are entitled to a federal tax credit of 15 percent of qualifying pension income up to $2,000 of pension income for the year. In Quebec, a credit for up to 20 percent of qualifying pension income up to a limit of $1,000 of pension income is available to persons 65 and over.

Qualifying pension income does not include the Canada Pension Plan, Old Age Security, and the Guaranteed Income Supplement. Qualifying pension income includes private pension income from life annuities. For people 65 and over or who receive payments as a result of the death of a spouse, it includes annuities created out of RRSPs or deferred profit-sharing plans, a payment from a Registered Retirement Income Fund, or the income component of an annuity. To make the most of this credit, you should have at least $2,000 of qualifying pension income a year and another $2,000 for a spouse.

Caregivers

A tax credit worth up to $623 is available for caregivers who provide care in the home for elderly or infirm relatives. The credit is reduced if the income of the person receiving care is over $13,726 and ceases when the income of that person exceeds $17,745. The credit can be claimed by only one person in the home of the infirm person. Thus if someone else in the home claims the credit for an infirm dependent over age 18, no one else may obtain the credit.

Home Support in Quebec

Quebec provides for a refundable tax credit for the home support of people age 70 or older. The credit equals 25 percent of eligible expenses paid to obtain designated home support services. The credit has a maximum annual benefit of $3,750. If the expense also meets the test for a Quebec medical expense credit, it cannot be claimed for both purposes. It is necessary, therefore, to determine which form of credit is the more beneficial.

Pension Income Splitting

In announcements made on October 31, 2006, then Minister of Finance Jim Flaherty announced, among other things, that certain pension income could be split between people married or equivalent to married. The income that is eligible for splitting is that which would be eligible for the Pension Income Tax Credit, namely, periodic payments from a registered pension plan and, providing that the recipient is at least age 65, income from Registered Retirement Income Funds and the interest component of annuities. The non-interest component of annuities, it should be said, would be a return of capital immune from taxation.

Pension income from the CPP/QPP and OAS and the Guaranteed Income Supplement is not eligible for splitting under the Minister's announcement because it can be split upon application for reasons of divorce or preference of qualified persons. OAS income is regarded by the federal government as a statutory and personal benefit.

Under the pension splitting provisions, there is no actual division of underlying assets. All that happens is that the recipient can allocate income of up to half of qualifying amounts and resulting tax liability to a spouse or person equivalent to spouse. Application to split qualified income has to be made via CRA form T 1032, "Joint Election to Split Pension Income," and both the splitter and the person receiving the split must agree to the process by filing the election on or before the due date of the applicable tax return.

Pension income splitting reduces the net income of the person doing the split and increases the net income of the person receiving the split. There are, therefore, consequences for the OAS clawback, qualification for provincial age and medical expense credits, and payments and tax instalment requirements. Thus the split mechanism needs to be watched carefully. Splitting would tend to be advantageous when the person receiving the split does not wind up with a greater exposure to tax than the person doing the split. In other words, if the split pushes the income of the recipient over the clawback threshold of $64,718 in 2008, then the recipient spouse could be subject to the clawback. There may still be a net benefit, however, provided that the split does not reduce the federal age credit discussed above. The complexities of the splitting process are enough to drive those contemplating splits to consult with tax professionals.

Dividend Income

The structure of the tax calculations for personal income tax gives perverse power to dividends to reduce the age credit and the clawback. That's because dividends from eligible Canadian corporations are grossed up or inflated by 45 percent when calculating net income. That can boost net income to a point at which these benefits are impaired or lost, even though the dividend tax credit may restore much of the dividend later on in the tax calculation process. The gross-up does not affect capital gains, interest income, or earned income. While the tax rate applicable to dividend income may be half that on interest and earned income, neither interest nor earned income are exaggerated for purposes of calculating net income.

The effect of the dividend tax credit on federal programs to benefit retirees looks like robbing Peter to pay Paul. If the federal government wants to ensure that retirees get the full benefits of statutory programs that enhance the incomes of retirees, Parliament ought to compensate for the effect of dividends on seniors' benefits. Splitting can help mitigate the erosion of benefits, but in yet another example of what may be benevolently regarded as a mere oversight, the mitigation doesn't work if there is no one with whom to split. In other words, elderly folks with living spouses or equivalent to spouse can reduce the income erosion of having dividends. Those who have no living spouse or equivalent are, as the expression goes, up the creek.

Chapter 8

What Are You Going to Do with All Those Years?

It is a paradox that with mandatory retirement in decline throughout Canada, ever more people want to give early retirement a try. The reasons for what appears to be a movement toward early retirement lie in economics and one insurance company's marketing strategy.

Retirement at age 65, once a standard across the country, has become an antique. The idea is not quite dead, but the rule of "65 and out" is now seen as age discrimination in the workplace.

Ontario moved to ban compulsory retirement in December 2006. The province passed an amendment to the provincial Human Rights Code that makes it illegal to impose mandatory retirement on employees.

Similar rules were in effect in Alberta, Manitoba, Prince Edward Island, Nunavut, Quebec, the Yukon, and the Northwest Territories. But the Ontario law added authority and weight to the national trend, for as the centre of manufacturing activity and most corporate head offices in the country, it turned the trend, which had been started in provinces with smaller populations and smaller provincial economies, into a national fact.[1] However, the presumption that an employee has the right to work regardless of age does not preclude an employer from dismissing, suspending, or transferring an employee for good and sufficient reasons.

Several provinces have limited the force of compulsory retirement by defining situations or ages to which it may be applied. In British Columbia, older employees are protected against discrimination based on age. In Nova Scotia, mandatory retirement at age 65 is not considered to be discriminatory under that province's human rights legislation, provided that such a policy is applied uniformly in the workplace. In New Brunswick, Alberta, Prince Edward Island, and Newfoundland and Labrador, termination of employment because of the terms of a bona fide retirement or pension plan is not necessarily considered to be discriminatory under provincial human rights legislation. If there is no such plan, employees can file a complaint for age discrimination under provincial human rights legislation without regard to age. Ironically, at the federal level, it is not a discriminatory practice to terminate a person's employment because that person has reached the normal age of retirement for employees working in similar positions. In those cases, the employer is permitted to uphold mandatory retirement.[2]

As *When Can I Retire?* heads to press, the Supreme Court of Canada has reviewed compulsory retirement. A worker in a New Brunswick mine owned by the Potash Corp. of Saskatchewan was given notice that he had to retire when he turned 65 in 2004. He complained to the New Brunswick Human Rights Commission. In its mid-July 2008 ruling, the Supreme Court held that mandatory retirement, which has been extensively curtailed across Canada, is lawful if the employer has designed a retirement plan that goes into effect at age 65. Companies are immune from penalties for discrimination if they can show that their pension plans were created in good faith and not as a way to limit employees' rights. Paradoxically, Potash Corp. ended involuntary retirement in November 2007. The decision appears to validate exceptions to rules against involuntary retirement that are also in effect in Alberta, Prince Edward Island, and Newfoundland and Labrador.[3]

The compulsion to quit work at a specific age is ending, the result of both human rights initiatives and the recognition in law of the fact that many people at 60 and 70 or older remain healthy and productive. Yet rather than take full advantage of the right to work, some people are trying to retire as early as age 50. Some even want to quit work in their forties. Why?

What's Behind the Desire to Retire Early

The explanation is simply this: It seems possible to do. Rising asset values, especially the real estate boom that boosted the prices of homes across Canada, gave people the feeling that they were affluent. Defined benefit pension plans that assure retirees that their incomes will pace inflation may be the privilege of ever fewer people, but the rising prices of shares on the Toronto Stock Exchange and other bourses around the world supported the feeling of affluence. The appearance of affluence seems to have generated a bandwagon effect. For every person who retires at age 60 or 65, there are many others who would like to give retirement a try at a much earlier age.

It is all the more ironic that the wish to retire early is flourishing in the face of the decline of defined benefit pension plans. Moreover, with interest rates having slipped from double-digit levels in the 1980s and high single-digit levels in the 1990s to low single digits today, it is no longer possible to live on a string of guaranteed investment certificates. Retirees are forced to take some risks with their investments and those who decide to quit work are clearly adding to their economic risks.

The explanation for the rising popularity of early retirement thus rests on the widespread belief that it can be done. The London Life "Freedom 55" marketing campaign, mentioned earlier, seems to have made a great many Canadians believe that it's possible to quit work with no risk a decade before the mandatory retirement age, usually 65. The plan, which trumpeted the idea that with appropriate savings and investment plans, you could quit work at 55, has become a catchphrase and a concept that people believe is real enough to work.

For some, perhaps a lucky few, it may work, but for the majority of Canadians, Freedom 55 is a myth with numbers. Says Caroline Nalbantoglu, a registered financial planner with PWL Capital Corp. in Montreal, "Forget it! The idea that average Canadians can build up enough capital at age 55 to sustain their lives for another 30 years is just a dream."

What to Do with the Years Ahead

Retirement at any age requires three things, call them the three Ms, to be successful: (1) money—enough of it, (2) motive—a reason for retiring, and (3) meaning—a sense of fulfillment in the time away from work. You can have these three things at any age, but for most people, it takes time to get them. After all, it takes time to generate retirement savings, a life of work to make non-work meaningful, and some life lived to want to spend time reflecting on it.

Decades ago, when life expectancy was shorter than it is today and fewer workers lived to age 65 or even age 60, what to do with the remaining few years of life was not a problem. Workers who made it to the mandatory retirement point were often exhausted by four or five decades of hard labour. They might leave work in poor health and just be glad to be able to sit in a rocking chair and watch their grandchildren play.

Retiring in middle age at 55 or even earlier raises the question of what you will do with years of good health. Without a job to go to, many retirees have no reason to get up in the morning. Those who got their identities from work may find it tough to go out into the world as the newly, even if voluntarily, unemployed.

Psychologist Nancy K. Schlossberg has produced a classification of retiree attitudes based on work habits.[4] In her breakdown, there are:

1. Continuers, who use existing skills and interests from their work
2. Adventurers, who start entirely new endeavours
3. Searchers, who explore options through trial and error
4. Easy Gliders, who like unscheduled time
5. Involved Spectators, who care about the world but remain somewhat disengaged
6. Retreaters, who take time out or abandon active involvement in community life

QUESTION: What are some important attributes of a successful retirement?

ANSWER: The three Ms: (1) money—enough of it, (2) motive—a reason for non-work, and (3) meaning—a sense of fulfillment in the time away from work.

The American psychologist Abraham Maslow (1908–1970) is famous for having identified a hierarchy of human needs. In his conception, human needs have layers: food, air, water, and sex at the base; then safety needs, including security and stability; then social needs to belong and to have love and acceptance; and, at the top, the need to fulfill oneself and to become all that one can be. In retiring, many people forsake the highest level of the Maslow order, giving up identity and purpose and pushing themselves down one or two levels to merely safe existence.

This is precarious territory. Without a purpose, retirement is a void. What that purpose is or should be is an individual choice. It can be a love of golf, a desire to travel, to do volunteer work in a developing country, to study, to be an artist or pursue a hobby, or to devote your life to a religious order or to take a more secular path of helping others. The point is that there should be a goal or a plan of positive activity or action. Just quitting because it seems possible is not only foolish, it is precarious.

Constructing a Successful Retirement

Retirement is usually understood to mean that you are stepping from a place or time when you must do things others want to a time or place when it's you who will decide what to do and when to do it. Planning retirement as the leaving without considering the arriving is procedurally incomplete.

Retirement counselling books in the inspirational style try to convey a "you can do it if you believe you can" message. We'll skip this hype and concentrate instead on what a useful retirement plan should be.

1. Fulfilling: You need a desire to do things and a plan to do them in succession as you age.

2. Affordable: A life of cruising works only if there is a budget to support it.
3. Engaging: The retirement plan should provide a way to make meaningful use of the free time you will have on your hands.
4. Adaptable: If one plan does not work out, there should be another to take its place.

My weekly column in the Toronto *Globe and Mail*, Financial Facelift, receives requests for retirement plans more than for any other topic. Most of those requests for retirement plans focus on retirement at ages before 65, some as early as 40. Few of those requests specify what the intended retiree is going to do with the decades ahead. Among people who do have specific retirement vocations, few have tested them. Most people will not buy a car without a test drive. Ironically, the majority of retirement-focused correspondents I hear from are willing to give up much more than the price of a car on an untested desire to step into the world after work without a vocational compass.

Ask yourself what you really want to do with 10 or 20 or more years after the end of your job or career. If you have a hobby or sport, it can provide a basis for pleasant hours. But will that fill every day? How else will you spend days and nights without work? If you leave the question open and expect to come up with an idea once you have retired, you could be in for disappointment. Leisure, after all, gets meaning from the work to which it is an alternative.

Many retirees see their life after work as a progression. If your career can be shifted from gaining to giving within the professional space, the transition to non-work will be that much easier. For example,

The businessperson with a string of successes can teach others how a career can be fruitful and profitable. He or she can speak in a formal educational environment, perhaps as a lecturer at a business school or in a university.

The pharmacist who finishes a career behind the dispensary counter can join a consumer group as a specialist in drug-related issues.

The civil engineer can become a consultant to governments concerned with the safety of infrastructure.

The retail services employee can join a consumer group as an arbitrator of disputes.

The florist can work with nursing homes to make spaces more agreeable with his or her green thumb.

The carpenter can move from framing houses for contractors to working with a charitable group to build or repair homes for the poor.

The school teacher who leaves active classroom work may migrate to association work or go to a developing country to help set up schools.

The investment banker can migrate to a university or foundation to help run its endowment.

Each of these post-career moves represents an intelligent shift of skills from one accomplishment to another. It may be an extension of what the person was doing before, but the environment is likely to be different, the goals different, and the compensation as much or more psychological than financial.

On the other hand, in the new environment, there may be no more performance evaluations and hierarchies of managers to satisfy, more direct access to people being helped, and perhaps different feelings of rewards.

Is this just idealistic thinking? No, not at all. In my field, which is financial analysis, many opportunities are posted for work with international bodies. There are ads for related positions in *The Financial Times* of London, in *The Economist*, and in several major Canadian newspapers—just to name a few situations that are available.

> **Exercise:** Think through a retirement plan of, say, 20 years' length. What do you plan to do with that time? Will you golf, spend time with kids, have a part-time job, travel? Try to imagine two decades of vacation. How does it feel?

Before deciding on a post-career path and breaking ties with your current employment, do the smart thing: Take a test drive. If the work you want to do is in the tropics, for example, take an extended leave or even a month's holiday in the place. Check out what life is like for ordinary folks and expatriates. There are pleasant countries where foreigners are welcomed and others where foreigners are seen as opportunistic targets for kidnapping. Beware, be guided by intensive research on your goals, and be astute enough to realize that not every change of scenery is worth its cost.

Mapping Out Your Retirement

The general goal of retiring at 50 or 55, 60 or 65 has to be seen in terms of both the life you plan to leave and the next life in retirement. Among the issues to be considered are the strictly financial problems. They include the following:

Payment of debts. List the obligations you have to satisfy from mortgages, lines of credit, credit card debts, old loans, car payments, business debts, and promises to children and grandchildren. Add it up. Are you able to pay off the costs of your old life and move on to the next?

Cash flow in retirement. Stack up your sources of income from those that are certain, such as government pensions, to those that are uncertain or variable, such as returns from Registered Retirement Income Funds. Over time, more may come on stream. Are they payable when you are abroad? CPP and QPP pensions are payable without condition to qualified persons. OAS/GIS pensions have Canadian residency requirements. OAS payments to Canadian residents with less than 20 years of residence in Canada may be suspended after six months of absence and not resumed until the recipient returns to Canada. If a position one takes abroad involves payment for services rendered, will that income, when reported to the Canada Revenue Agency, trigger the Old Age Security clawback, thus possibly neutralizing some of the financial benefits of alternative or part-time employment in retirement? This is pencil work and it is worth doing carefully.

Management of affairs. Can you monitor your accounts with the office and computing resources you have at home? If you go abroad, will it be possible to monitor accounts from the destination? Are there sufficient internet resources to allow use of the internet to check accounts and pay bills? Can it be done by phone or by fax? Are you going to be comfortable with the level of security available in the destination? Remember that while e-mail can be encrypted, phone and fax is much harder to turn into code that others cannot read.

Health care. If you are thinking of being out of Canada for extended periods, will you be able to obtain affordable travel medical insurance? Rates for seniors tend to be much higher than for younger people. Is the medical system in the place to which you anticipate retiring going to be adequate for your health needs? This can be as problematic as finding a gynecologist in Nepal where the standard is traditional Tibetan medicine or as relatively easy as finding fresh fruit in the Yukon—it's there, but expensive.

Compliance with local law. Good intentions can come to bad ends if your plans conflict with local custom in other countries. Local school teachers in some places may resent the presence of outsiders. Within Canada, there may be agreements that make it essential for anyone doing carpentry to be a member of a certain union. Doctors leaving one province after a career and wishing to work as locums in the new province may find there are elaborate licensing conditions to be met, insistence on reviews of credentials, or insurance standards to be met. What seems easy and reasonable in theory can turn out to be monstrously difficult in practice. How easy is it to get money from Canada? Local postal service in the developing world may take weeks or months to deliver mail from abroad. Postal inspectors may be known to post informal duties on money from abroad, that is, to demand bribes before allowing money to move to its recipient.

Is the local banking system workable? Canada has one of the world's fastest and more dependable cheque-clearing systems. In other countries, including the United States, it can take weeks to clear foreign cheques.

Will you be double taxed on income? If you cease to be a resident of Canada, Canada will stop taxing your income in general, though it may impose such things as recovery tax, which is like the clawback on Old Age Security payments. Some countries are exempt from the requirement to report world income for purposes of the recovery tax. In others, the entire amount of OAS will be withheld if an OAS Return of Income report is not filed by April 30 of each year. If OAS will be a significant part of your income, you need to research this branch of tax law by contacting the following department:

International Operations Department
333 River Road
Ottawa, ON K1A 0L4
http://www.hrdc.gc.ca
1-800-277-9914 (Canada and the U.S.)
613-957-1954—collect calls are accepted from outside Canada
e-mail: isp-psr.mail-poste@hrdc.gc.ca

Living abroad may become more expensive if the country in question taxes Canadian cash flows as income, even though Canada may regard them as nontaxable returns of capital from investments. The problem of double taxation and the related issue of trying to get money back from foreign tax authorities can turn what might seem a prosperous foreign life into a period of poverty. If you plan to retire to any foreign country, talk to a foreign tax specialist with a major accounting firm in Canada. This advice may be expensive, but it could turn out to be even more costly not to have taken it and made an unwise and subsequently costly move out of Canada. See also Chapter 10 for more detailed information on selected foreign destinations.

What do others who are doing what you have in mind have to say? Talk to expatriates in the foreign country you want to live in.

Talk to folks who act for various associations welcoming new Canadians to communities. Do they get feelings of fulfillment? Do they get paid? Are there compensating benefits for lack of payment? If it is a group activity, do you like the group?

What will it cost to return to Canada or to your children or grandchildren? If you are staying at home, forget the question. If you plan to teach English in Tibet, the question is germane. Note that the ultra-cheap, out-of-season airfares that Air Canada and discount carriers in Europe offer to people in Calgary or Toronto may not be available to people in Kazakhstan. Assume nothing, try to go where there is competitive air travel, safe trains, and decent roads. After all, the romance of the unknown may be adventure for the young. If you are old and have a heart condition, the stresses of living abroad and trying to get back to Canada for medical treatment could be deadly.

Ownership of property. This is not really an issue in Canada. You may have to pay annual licence fees and insurance to run a car, but the value of the car is not subject to any sort of annual capital tax. But in other countries, residents may be taxed on their wealth. France, for example, has an annual wealth tax on worldwide assets over approximately $1 million.[5] The tax is controversial and has driven many wealthy residents of France to countries that do not tax wealth on top of taxing the income that built up that wealth.

What will be the disposition of property at death? Find out if the legal system in the country will accept a Canadian will both in law and in practice. The assumption that you can convey an estate in Canada to a grandchild may not work if the country in which you are living has high death duties and formal or informal ways of enforcing them. Informal taxation, that is, forced bribery, is not a major issue in western Europe. It can be a very large issue in some developing countries. The way out of this problem may be to put assets for others into trusts with conditions for transfer at the testator's death. Lawyers charge for this vital work and the costs of this kind of financial protection have to be added to the total costs of retirement in certain chosen locations.

Planning Your Days

The sudden release from the rhythms of pre-retirement life that begin with the commute to work and end with dinner at a fixed time each evening can be exhilarating or distressing.

Charting retirement day by day beforehand is a discipline that forces you to avoid the assumption that not going to work will be fun. No doubt, the absence of the daily commute will be fun for a while. But with the workplace gone, your business cards trashed, your occupational or professional identity lost, and your purpose for getting through the day now in question, a daily calendar is essential. The German philosopher Goethe said, "None are so hopelessly enslaved as those who falsely believe they are free." Without the daily routine of work and relaxation at the end of the day, life can turn into misery. Certainly, this is an individual thing. Some retirees will welcome the opportunity to spend the morning with the *New York Times* and the afternoon with the *Wall Street Journal*, lunchtime at church or an afternoon in a yoga class. Some will take pleasure in finally being able to fulfill that long-held dream of renovating the basement or rebuilding the deck. Others will golf when the weather permits, have a drink after the game, then move to a drink before the game, and then, eventually, give up the golf and just keep on drinking.[6] Alcoholism is a vast problem among the retired, growing in severity when a spouse passes away, deepening as sense of abandonment extends to asking philosophical questions of life and destiny. In working years, we usually have no time to ponder these things. In retirement, philosophical speculations can turn into an abyss of despair.

The alternative, of course, is to keep busy. The way to test your ability to do this is to lay out your days with calendars. What will you do on Monday mornings? Will you have obligations to satisfy? They can be self-generated, for example, a need to shop or clean the house. Or contractual if there is a job like delivering meals to shut-ins. They can be spiritual, as in going to mass. Or pleasurable, like a visit to grandchildren on fixed days of the week. The point is to fill your days with meaningful activity, your evenings with friends, your weekends with travel or other friends, and your vacations from the extended vacation of retirement with special opportunities.

The great New York Yankee manager Yogi Berra once said, "If you don't know where you are going, you can wind up somewhere else." In that seemingly simplistic statement is the truth of retirement planning.

Chapter Summary

Just as compulsory retirement is ending, many middle-aged people are trying to retire at age 55. There is no right or wrong time to retire, but there are personal goals that retirement should meet. First, it should be within your means; second, there should be a good reason for retiring; and third, there should be meaning in retirement. These things can be estimated, planned, and assessed in advance by some introspection. In every case, whenever one retires, it is vital to future happiness that the time after work be more than just an escape. It should provide for personal fulfillment as well.

Chapter 9

Time and Certainty

In a financial sense, retirement is a work in progress. As we've discovered, the idea that you can produce one plan to go into effect at age 50 or 60 or 70 and stick with it for a few decades is confident to a fault. The future is unlikely to unfold in some constant way, so you cannot plan for every eventuality. The problem, in a nutshell, is that we tend to see the present as the way of the future. It seldom turns out that way.

You know by now that the longer the period of retirement or, if you prefer, the earlier the time of retirement, the harder it is to see ahead. A few examples will illustrate the problem.

As Time Expands, Certainty Declines

In 1962, interest rates were in low single digits. U.S. Treasury bonds with 10-year maturities paid 4.12 percent. In Canada, commercial certificates of deposit paid 3.25 to 4.75 percent, depending on the month. Twenty years later in 1982, 10-year U.S. Treasuries had coupon rates of 14.19 percent. Two-year Government of Canada bonds paid as much as 16.40 percent.[1] The leap of more than 10 percentage points was unprecedented. The

cause, the American policy of financing the Vietnam war by inflation, could not have been known in the early days of the Kennedy
administration when President Johnson's war was being planned.
But retirees with no debts and cash in their pockets found they had
more nominal buying power in the early 1980s when cash became
the best asset one could have.

You might protest that inflation in the 1970s had robbed them
and everyone else of purchasing power, but in the 1981–1982 cost-
of-living squeeze, when consumer prices were rising at double-digit
rates in Canada, investors had the chance to buy government
bonds that paid 12 percent for 30 years. It was an opportunity that
came once in many generations.

As the millennium began, Nortel Networks was regarded by
analysts as the centre of the technological universe. Its stock sold
north of $120 per share. Today, as I am writing this chapter
just eight years later, Nortel shares have been trading in a $5 to
$6 range.

Nortel was not an ephemeral investment. Indeed, it was at one
time at the core of many institutional portfolios. Nortel has moved
to the outer orbits of large cap corporations. Everyone knows it's
there, but a lot of portfolio managers don't bother with it. U.S.
Treasury bonds remain important and unavoidable in public and
private finance.

If there is no perfect, guaranteed financial plan with assets
geared to support foreseeable expenses, what can you do? The task
is challenging, but there are, in fact, ways to cope. You won't need
a degree in computer science or a background in fancy math. You
will need to focus on the concept of transitory risk.

Transitory risk is the equivalent of day-to-day changes in stock
prices. It is customary to look at the day's trading and compare the
cost of a stock to the previous day. The daily ups and downs can

drive you mad. But over a period of years or decades, good stocks show steady progress. Indeed, if we used just the moving average of five-year stock prices, we would see smooth climbing values and we would have no worries at all. At least for most stocks—Nortel being an exception.

The Progression of Income and the Decline of Certainty

Lowest certainty	Windfall income from inheritances & lotteries	Rising income
	Commodities (high risk), stocks (medium risk),	
	Corporate bonds (lower risk)	
	Tailored retirement funds	
	RRSPs, RRIFs, LIFs, LRIFs	
	Defined benefit pension plans	
	Annuities, life insurance payouts	
Highest certainty	OAS, GIS, CPP, QPP, government bonds	Declining income

The Dependability of Assets and Income

Some things are certain, none more so than the ability of governments to pay pensions. Old Age Security may be income-tested by the clawback, but it will be paid. Moreover, OAS and the Canada and Quebec Pension Plans are indexed to track the Consumer Price Index, so their purchasing power should remain intact no matter what happens to inflation rates.

Annuities and life insurance contracts issued by major life companies in Canada are solid. Assuris, the industry's benefit guarantee organization, stands ready to make good within limits if a member company that has entered into an annuity or life insurance contract defaults.

Invested assets outside of registered plans rise or fall with market forces. They are not certain in the same sense as government-funded pensions. These assets can be put into a time frame to make planning retirement a financially meaningful exercise.

First, we have to deal with the question that most people ask: How can we be certain that we can afford to retire? No financial planner can truthfully say that variable income that depends on how mutual funds or stocks or bonds work out over various time periods will balance with expenses that will fluctuate in their susceptibility to inflation. The planning process can set out income projections subject to stated assumptions and, indeed, financial planning software helps planners work out combinations of CPP/QPP, OAS, company pensions, and RRSP growth for target years. But these planning projections are just the outcome of equations based on assumptions. Constructing the equations for the scores of variables in a process of balancing income and expense is the difficult part.

Consistent with the idea that planning is a work in progress, it is better to be modest in your ambitions and set plans for tiers of years. You can make assumptions about the first five years, the second five years, and so on. This process recognizes what is relatively certain and what is not very certain in the planning process.

If 60 percent or more of your retirement income will consist of defined benefit and indexed pensions from OAS, CCP/QPP, annuities, and company plans, you have a good chance of predicting your income flow within reasonable limits. You still have to make assumptions about the rate of inflation ahead, but you can adopt the consensus view of 2 to 3 percent for the next three decades. That is what the bond market is saying and it is usually, though not always, a good predictor of the future.

With a fairly strong indicator of income, you can plan the level of expense you can afford. Leave some wiggle room. You don't need to have a one-to-one relationship of income to expense. Set the income to 130 percent of expenses or, if you prefer, ensure that anticipated expenses do not exceed 77 percent of income. The greater the excess coverage of expenses, the more secure your retirement will be. But this seemingly obvious suggestion contains a subtle point: The more variable the income, the greater the excess coverage of expenses has to be. Thus a portfolio of mutual funds that are structured to generate capital gains from smart stock-picking is going to be more variable in returns and distributions than one that has nothing but government bonds or perhaps a blend of bonds and large cap, diversified stocks. If you set expenses at half of expected income, you should have a substantial margin of safety.

The younger you are when retirement begins, the more conservative the planning process has to be. Likewise, if you want to leave money to children or to an estate, you need to ensure that the money is not eroded by having to spend beyond the plan. If the intent is to leave 10 percent of an estate or a fixed sum, that has to be protected in the planning process.

Your taste for risk also enters into the equation. If you are a short-term risk averter, you probably reject high levels of stock exposure in favour of fixed income assets. The problem with this approach is that, over time, inflation is sure to erode the purchasing power of returns from bonds and preferred stocks. If you have a portfolio with 60 percent or more fixed income assets that are not inflation-protected, you will wind up with significantly reduced spending power as time goes on. However, it does not follow that returns grow as risk increases. The theory that risk and return go together has no time measure. In other words, if assets or income is very unpredictable, the gains may not appear in a given time period or, indeed, even in your lifetime.

On the other hand, if you are risk-tolerant, you can hold high levels of common stocks and stock mutual funds. You will have a good deal of volatility in periodic returns, but over the long run, a diversified portfolio of stocks should rise in value and pace inflation.

Budgeting income and expense takes not only good pencil work, but wisdom. Income can usually be raised by adding risk. But risk is anathema when it comes to long-term income for retired persons. If you have a diversified portfolio of low- or reasonable-fee mutual funds, some stocks with strong and rising dividends, and high-quality bonds, your income should be stable and sustainable. Trading on short-term trends adds risk and, as financial analysts know, portfolio turnover and return are inversely related. Buy quality investments and let them ride, selling only when fundamentals turn adverse. Trading on day-to-day price movements is perilous.

Beware retirement plans and products that increase your debt. Some investment dealers and mutual fund salespeople suggest increasing income by borrowing against a house that is debt-free. If an insured mortgage costs 5 percent and the portfolio they are selling is supposed to produce 10 percent a year, the proposition seems foolproof. The flaw in the argument is that the house mortgage is riskless to the lender, who will be paid even if you default and you are at risk with a portfolio of stocks or other negotiable assets. When you factor in risk, borrowing against a home is potentially a way to foreclosure. Moreover, if the interest rate charged on the house mortgage were to rise substantially, you could find the mortgage, which was once easy to service, unaffordable. And interest rates are going to rise either from cyclical factors or, perhaps, the desire of foreign central banks that hold huge amounts of U.S. Treasury bonds to get paid for the declines in

American currency against the Euro and other major currencies. That could force up the entire structure of interest rates charged by Canadian lenders. Will it happen? We don't know, though there are intelligent voices claiming that it will.[2]

QUESTION: What is the relationship between income and risk?

ANSWER: In general, potential income rises with risk, but in a practical sense, it may take years or a lifetime to realize gains. For retirees and others with relatively short time frames, it pays to make substantial investments in lower risk, lower return but predictable assets.

The composition of income and expense is likely to change over time. In this table, for someone who retires at age 60, we can see the evolution of spending and income with the assumption that expense will be no more than 70 percent of income.

Age	Variable (non CPP/QPP & OAS) assets	Expense composition
60	40% stocks, 60% fixed income, continued savings and asset building	Substantial recreational spending, new car every x years, foreign travel
65	35% stocks, 65% fixed income, asset accumulation ends, OAS begins	Recreational spending declines, higher supplemental health insurance & drug costs, less travel, no more new cars
70	30% stocks, 70% fixed income, RRSP used to buy an annuity with remainder saved for RRIF	Travel now infrequent, entertainment declines, creation of a trust for children, grandchildren
75	25% stocks, 75% fixed income including annuity payments	Travel spending slows further, little entertainment outside the home, car sold, more spending on gifts for children & others

High Yield Can Mean Big Trouble

In this example, the level of fixed income assets rises by 5 percent every five years as stock and stock mutual fund exposure drops a similar amount. But if our subject were to begin retirement at, say, age 75 and have no plans to leave a legacy for others, he or she would do well to put 75 percent or even 80 percent of assets into fixed income assets. In old age, the last thing you need is portfolio destruction caused by a falling market.

Bond returns can plummet as much as stock returns. When the majority of today's middle-aged money managers were born, fixed income meant government bonds. There were stiff rules for pension fund and trust fund trustees that required them to put their beneficiaries' money into government bonds and nothing but. In the mid- and later 1970s, interest rates began to rise. Government of Canada bonds with three- to five-year maturities posted average yields of 2.56 percent in January 1951, 4.60 percent in January 1961, 5.37 percent in January 1971, and 13.14 percent in January 1981. In September 1981, yields got up to 18.77 percent before an intervention by the Bank of Canada that began a long slide down to low single digits in 2004. From April to August 2004, Canada's bank rate was a modest 2.25 percent. That slide in interest rates was great for borrowers but not so good for yield-hungry investors.

Standing by was an industry that was ready to jack up yields on debt instruments. You could buy so-called preferred securities with names like BOATS and BATS. These were not quite preferred shares and not quite bonds. They qualified as low-grade unsecured preferred stock. Though mostly issued by chartered banks and senior corporations, they came with a few percentage points of yield boost over the issuers' high-grade bonds. Then there were mortgages and credit card receivables packaged for the institutional market. Engineered to get triple A ratings (sometimes with a good deal of gaming of the ratings systems, as it turns out), these asset-backed certificates offered about 30 basis points (there are 100 basis points in one percentage point) of yield boost over Government of Canada bonds of the same term. Investors plunged, as they had a decade earlier when Drexel Burnham Lambert junk bond wunderkind Michael Milken persuaded the world that risky debt was really safe enough to buy and that the extra yield on junk would more than cover a few defaults. In fact, Milken had glossed over a central fact that concerns us: Dicey fixed income assets, like fruit, take time to rot.

Milken was convicted in 1989 of six counts of racketeering and was sentenced to pay a $500-million fine, which he easily did, and to serve 10 years in jail. He served two years in jail, was released, and became a philanthropist. He walked away from the financial disaster he had sown. Of 104 small companies whose junk bonds he sold, 24 percent defaulted on their debt or were bankrupt by 1990.[3] He left many investors in ruins.

Junk bond schemes and today's collapse of part of the asset-backed commercial paper market have a common thread that is vital to understand in retirement planning: High yields that appear to flow from unusual fixed income products attract more money, which competes away some of those yields through an ordinary bidding process as more people toss more money at the new stuff. Then early entrants may start to take their money out. If the product operates with borrowed money on leverage, the lenders may get nervous. There are more demands for cash and late investors may wind up with nothing. This is the mechanism of the Ponzi scheme, in which early investors are paid not with returns, but with the cash of later investors. What all these schemes have in common is that it is time that turns apparent gold to dust.

There is a saying in financial circles that pigs get slaughtered. It is almost certainly true in judging high-yield products. If the yield boost of some novel fixed income device over top-quality government bonds is huge, there has to be an associated elevation of risk. That risk may have delayed consequences, but it is almost certainly there.

> **Exercise:** Review your own experience in order to make a list of assets that have had a potential of high returns but that produced disappointing results. You should be able to come up with at least half a dozen, perhaps including lottery tickets, dot-com stocks, perhaps Labour Sponsored Venture Capital Funds, and other mutual funds.

Should You Die Broke?

Financial planners often assume that one should have spent one's last dollar by the moment of death. This is considered efficient planning in some circles. The idea is rooted in the life-cycle concept in economics, that is, that people should save and spend in a fashion that maximizes the value of the money they earn. So you should save in earning years and spend in the later years. The conclusion that you should be totally tapped out at the moment of death is the inevitable conclusion of the process.

Life does not always follow economic laws. Moreover, dying without a dime is precarious planning. The moment of death usually cannot be timed. The risk of this "broke at death" concept is that lengthening life expectancy may make the possibility of terminal bankruptcy a reality. It would be far better to plan to keep 10 percent or more of your financial assets into very old age, say 100 or even 110. That appears to be the limit of life today, though in a few decades there may be enough centenarians around to raise the probabilities of getting to 100 from obscure to realizable.

Moreover, those who have no money after the actuarial estimates of death, which currently averages 82 for men and 87 for women, may become burdens on their children or on their communities. Old age can be a tough time to endure; to be old and impoverished is all the worse.

The planning procedure for setting up a late-life reserve is quite easy. As long as you spend a few percent less than your total retirement cash flow, there should be a positive balance of cash flow. The younger you are, the closer you can shave the earning/spending margin for there is more time for the surplus to grow. This is really just a way of imposing discipline on a spending pattern. The discipline functions to create an emergency and survival fund so that you will be less likely to end your days broke.

There is an alternative to creating a reserve fund, but while simple in concept, it is harder in execution. If you own a home in retirement and run your cash reserves down, you can sell the house and use the money for expenses for the rest of your life. This strategy is especially useful for people who have the majority of their pension income coming from non-indexed sources that do not pace inflation. A house, in general, will rise in value with inflation.

The problem with using a home as an emergency or late-life reserve is that you can't sell it in bits. A home is a single thing. Sell it and you have to buy another or rent. If the rental market is efficient, the rental cost will equal housing costs that consist of the total cost of principal and interest. If paid in full without a mortgage, the cost is the price plus foregone interest on money tied up in the house. You will, therefore, gain just a temporary cash balance by selling the house. However, there is a tax-free gain that can be realized. The sale of a principal residence bears no capital gains taxes. If the gain is substantial and if you downsize, you could have a hefty surplus. The longer the time you held the house, the more likely and the larger that gain will be. Downsizing can work, provided that rents rising over time do not eat up your gains. It is usually safer to borrow against the house in a conventional mortgage or secured line of credit.

Whether you plan to maintain a financial reserve or to use a home as a final asset when others are expended, it is vital to go through the planning process.

Planning Gear

Planning future asset values and cash flows is a lot easier with the right tools. Several financial management companies have appropriate software for financial planners and even for people who just want to be bean counters. Among the more interesting sources of programs is the RRIFmetic system. Company president Steve Salter says, "The program can handle multiple cash flows, tax planning, retirement planning, and insurance planning." See http://www.fimetrics.com. A home user edition of the program sells for $99 plus taxes from Fimetrics Systems Ltd., 2338 Nelson Ave., West Vancouver, B.C. V7V 2R2, or call 1-800-663-4088. Other programs can be found at http://www.fiscalagents.com along with numerous articles pertinent to financial planning.

An Ongoing Enterprise

As one gets older, the end of life gets to be more a reality than a possibility. We have incentives to make wise spending decisions for the period after which we cease to earn income and have to rely on pension entitlements and our own assets.

We know there are too many variables at work that can devastate the best of retirement plans. The best way to set up a plan for review is to list the critical variables and assumptions. These are interest rates, rates of return on assets, ages of dependents, deferred tax obligations, and the condition of corporate pension funds in which you have a financial interest. The larger the asset as a fraction of a portfolio, the more critical it is to follow its free cash flow and profits. If you hold real estate, appraisals every five years are vital. And if you have flow-through investments or structured investments that defer taxes, it is essential to know the value of those obligations.

When reviewing financial plans, you can verify that company pensions are flowing in correct amounts, that your income is correctly structured in terms of splits, that the person sharing your pension flows has not been pushed into a higher bracket than your own, and that there are ways to reduce OAS clawback exposure—if that is an issue.

Most of all, you can review investment portfolio returns to ensure that the stocks and mutual funds you own are still serving their purpose. Check to see that mutual fund fees are reasonable or are at least rewarded by proportional performance.

Check to see if you have capital losses in taxable accounts that can be used to offset taxable capital losses. If you have business income from self-employment, ensure that you are taking proper—but not excessive—expense deductions.

Fees for financial planning and many financial advisory services are deductible from income if they are used as a way of generating income. A tax advisor can tell you if fees paid for planning reviews are deductible.

The goal of planning and of reviews should be to produce income and to do it with a level of risk appropriate to the age and assets of the retired person or the person headed for retirement. In general, when you are retired, you should not have a high level of exposure to overly volatile stocks. Government bonds and top-quality corporate bonds should be used to counterbalance equity risk. Cash can be held in high-interest savings accounts and GICs at chartered banks. As registered assets mature, it may be desirable to add annuity income, which you can never run out of, to pensions. That is a security building process.

Pension management is about investment accumulation running backwards. It is about paying out rather than paying in. But the underlying entitlements and discretionary assets remain at work. They need to be kept in sight and supervised. As Warren Buffett has said, "Investment must be rational; if you can't understand it, don't do it."[4]

Chapter Summary

Risk and return are linked, but time is the unknown element in the relationship. Given that retirees may not have decades for some investments to bloom, they should focus on having substantial parts of their total assets and income in low- or lower-risk investments, including annuities, government bonds, and defined benefit pension plans. The fraction of total assets in low-risk assets should also rise over time. The aim at the end of life should be to have some surplus that was used as a cushion for rainy days or for bequeathing to heirs. In relatively few cases is it wise to design a pension and investment system to run out of money at a fixed date. After all, most people do not pass away on schedule.

Chapter 10

Retiring to a Life Away from Canada

Retirement can be a way to escape ice-swept Canadian winters, buggy summers, and the swampy seasons in between. Many take the opportunity of not having to show up at the office to do just that. The patterns of escapism are familiar: Florida is popular with Canadians from coast to coast, but especially popular with Quebecers. Folks on the prairies tend to head south to Texas and Mexico. Those in the west choose Mexico too but also Panama. Some Canadians head to ancestral roots in India for inexpensive living. Others go to Israel for cultural or religious reasons. Europe is expensive, but for those who can afford a life of spas and champagne, Switzerland offers good order and negotiable taxes. For those who have abundant wealth, there is yachting on the Mediterranean. Finally, there are tax havens, some of which are developing nations in Central America that accept long-term tourists and new residents, charge little tax, but also provide relatively few social services.

It is not necessarily easy to get away from Canada. Indeed, the Canada Revenue Agency takes the view that you must be absent from Canada for two or more years to show an intent to end Canadian residence. Other indicia of intent to reside outside of Canada include where your permanent home is, where bank accounts are held, where credit cards are billed, where drivers are licensed, and where you go to church or synagogue, mosque or temple. Returning to Canada within the two-year period to reestablish residence raises the possibility that CRA will tax income earned in the interval since you left Canada. Even coming back to Canada to see family or do some business can raise the odds of being returned to Canada for tax purposes. See the CRA Interpretation Bulletin IT-221, "Determination of an Individual's Residence Status."[1]

Leaving Canada can be expensive. Canada has a so-called departure tax. It deems that all accrued capital gains are realized on departure for assumption of residence in another tax jurisdiction— in other words, even if you don't sell all your assets, including divesting yourself of investments, CRA treats you as if you had monetized them at market prices and then seeks to tax the gains theoretically harvested from the sale. Capital gains in Canadian corporations are subject to the tax, though Canadian real estate is not. Land and buildings remain in Canada, after all. Problems arise in the treatment of shares in small corporations that are not publicly traded. Shares must be appraised and, if not sold, the owner must post security for eventual payment with the Minister of Finance.

The intent of the law is to prevent people subject to Canadian income taxes avoiding taxes by moving to another country. The consequence of the departure tax is to accelerate the taxation of accrued gains in public companies, to force the sale of shares and perhaps control of smaller companies, and to leave the question of what security is acceptable to the Minister of Finance without a clear answer. The Minister presumably does not want to hold shares and become a stockholder in various companies. Lack of clarity adds one more layer of difficulty in moving out of Canada permanently.

Old Age Security and Canada and Quebec Pension Plan benefits can be paid to qualified persons living outside of Canada. OAS requires you to file annual returns to show your worldwide income.

Canada has tax treaties with threescore countries. Among other things, these treaties reduce or eliminate double taxation of government and other pensions and income. To obtain a determination of non-resident status it is necessary to submit CRA form NR73, Residency Determination. If you cease to be a resident of Canada as defined by CRA, you will not be required to file Canadian tax returns. But it may be useful to file a return in order to get a refund of certain withholding taxes.

> **Exercise:** Think about the negatives of life in Canada: high taxes, cold winters, and tremendous distances between some major cities. Try to break the issues down in financial terms. How much would you pay for perpetually warm weather? Would the savings in a tax haven finance life abroad? Check the cost of medical and hospital insurance in what appears to be a desirable country. Check if it has advanced medical and hospital services. Does the math add up to a good reason to leave? Can you afford it? And could you afford a house in Canada, a house or condo abroad, and all the travel in between?

Beneficiaries of pensions such as OAS, CPP, and QPP are usually taxed by the withholding of 25 percent of the payment in question. However, it is possible, depending on the country in which you are living, to obtain a lower rate by filing CRA NR5.

CRA has the forms at its offices and online at http://www.
cra-arc.gc.ca/E/pbg/tf/nr5. Rates vary by country of residence—for
example, from 25 percent on OAS payments in some countries
down to 0 percent for the United Kingdom. Check with CRA for
the country in question. Call the CRA international tax office at
1-613-952-3741 or write to the Canada Revenue Agency,
International Tax Services Office, Ottawa, ON K1A 1A8.

There are certainly people who can benefit from moving to
countries with no income taxes, such as the Caymans, or to
Barbados, where taxes are very low, but in general, Canadians get a
fair return on what we pay in taxes. That is not to say that we could
not get a better deal, that government waste could not be less, or
that Ottawa could not be more responsive to what people want
government to do. Nevertheless, we have a reasonable if not ideal
health insurance scheme and a sense of geopolitical security.
Canadian banks run one of the fastest cheque-clearing systems in
the world, food is relatively cheap in comparison to prices in other
industrialized countries, and we have almost no direct taxation of
wealth, save in probate fees on death, which are, even if irritating
to heirs, relatively minor.

Establishing residence in another country cuts you off from
Canadian health care. You can replace public health insurance with
private insurance, but the cost can be a few thousand dollars a
month—depending on your state of health and the type of insurance that is required.

A Few Countries to Consider

We cannot review all the countries in the world, but in the
following pages, we highlight several countries to which many
Canadian retirees go.

Australia

The appeal of life in this most arid of continents is not so much financial as it is the people and the land itself. The country has sweaty tropics in the north; it offers balmy and temperate weather in the south, the east, and in Tasmania; and is vibrant in its cultures both immigrant and aboriginal. There is animal life that simply does not exist in Canada. The place is fascinating, the people are terrific, but the immigration laws are challenging.

Getting into Australia is no cinch. For people over 55, the requirements include sponsorship under a state or territorial program. There are asset tests, requirements to make certain investments, and rules mandating obtaining health insurance

Once you are in, Australia provides a marvellous life. Retirees can work part-time. The country is as open to business investment and new ideas as Canada was 100 years ago. There are problems, of course: A drought has devastated much of the land. There is also an acclimatization problem, for the language Australians speak, which resembles English, can require weeks of familiarization and even translation for the novice. For the determined and the adventurous, it's worth investigating, Mate.

Israel

A move to Israel may be many things, but it is not a way to avoid taxation. Taxes are steeply progressive. Immigration assistance is widely available through public and private programs.

Life in Israel is perhaps more varied in its styles from religious communities to collective enterprise in the kibbutz setting to rather conventional urban life in Tel Aviv. There remain security issues characteristic of the Middle East. For those who go, settle, and get into the culture, the rewards are substantial. Some people feel a duty to return to their presumptive origins, others go to enjoy the robust life of the cities, still others to take part in the blend of resorts, to float on the Dead Sea—the lowest place on earth—to see where Jesus walked, or just to live in what amounts to the greatest collective shrine on the planet.

Mexico

Mexico—the name conjures up warmth and lavish resorts, Spanish colonial culture, spicy food, and extremes of wealth and poverty. What it comes down to is that there is something for everyone. Extended stays are possible with FM3 and FM2 permits, the former a visa that has to be renewed each year and the latter a permanent visa that allows the holder to work in the country.

The attractions of Mexico in a financial sense are a relatively low cost of living in comparison to Canada. Foreign residents pay no tax on their income in Mexico. If you own a home, property taxes are very modest. Utility bills are low and property and casualty insurance is also inexpensive. The country is immensely popular with older Canadians who flock to centres like Cuernevaca, a town just south of Mexico City.

The downside of Mexico is a high crime rate. Though the rate is perhaps no worse than in major cities in the United States or Canada, foreigners have been singled out for kidnapping. Others have been murdered in resort areas with police and tourism authorities going out of their way to stonewall Canadian relatives of victims and even Canadian criminal investigators and lawyers trying to find the murderers. The stories one hears about taking care in drinking the water are true. Extensive corruption in police forces, some members of which have been arrested en masse, is another issue. But with care and some time invested in learning

Spanish, you can stretch a Canadian pension income quite far. Still, for first-timers, it is prudent to join an international community of retirees and other expatriates, of which there are many.

The bottom line for Mexico is that for any level of income, you can live a little better and perhaps much better than you can in Canada. Year-round sunshine, less pollution except in Mexico City, fresh vegetables and fruit in every season at low prices, and terrific scenery and wonderful people make the country a favoured and quite reasonable destination for retirees. Culturally, if you can get into the language, literature, music, art, and history of the country, the experience can be exhilarating.

Panama

If the cost of living and the cost of complying with U.S. tax law is daunting (see below), then consider other destinations. Some countries actively seek Canadian retirees. Panama, for example, has good weather and offers retirees 50 percent off almost every public service and many private services including medical care, movies, mortgage rates, restaurants, and airfares.

There are other benefits of Panamanian residence: The Investment Stability Law, passed in 1998, protects foreign investors from any change in tax and customs laws and duties for a period of 10 years after an investment is registered. Residents of Panama pay no tax on foreign incomes. New arrivals who build a house have no property taxes to pay for 20 years. The cost of house construction is US$40 per square foot, a quarter of the cost in Canada. A maid can be hired for $120 to $160 per month in U.S. dollars, which are legal tender in Panama. Phone service is inexpensive, and personal tax on locally generated income ranges from 4 to 30 percent. There is a Value Added Tax of 5 to 10 percent on most products and services. Crime is an issue, but it is at a level that should not affect expatriates living in the country's fine high-rise condos. Some may complain that living in condos is an artificial way of life, but if an urban oasis in the rainforest is appealing, Panama is worth a visit.

Switzerland

There are much cheaper places to live than Switzerland, but there is one Swiss custom that makes it ideal for wealthy retirees: Swiss tax authorities are prepared to negotiate an annual lump-sum tax based on the rental value of one's home. It's called the *forfait fiscal* in French and the *Pauschalbesteurung* in German. It works like this: If you pay rent of, say, SFr. 3,000 per month (C$2,760) or SFr. 36,000 per year, your taxable annual estimated income will be five times Swiss annual rent or SFr. 180,000 and your tax would be 30 percent of that or SFr. 54,000 per year. That's about C$51,154. No one asks about your real income or your wealth. But if you live in a modest apartment, the presumptive income would fall and, with it, the tax. A small apartment in a Swiss village would allow for travel to many European locations. Switzerland is not a tax haven, contrary to what many think. But it is a haven of reasonable taxation.

Switzerland is also a highly developed country. Swiss police keep the crime rate down. Privacy is part of the national character. The food is excellent, the culture varies from one canton to another, and with France on the west, Italy on the South, Germany to the north, and Austria to the east, there is no chance of running out of culture or great places to go on weekends. For the sick, Swiss clinics are famous. For the rich, the boutiques and galleries of Zurich and Geneva provide great shopping. You won't get many bargains in Switzerland, but you do get a lot for what you pay.

United States

There are many good reasons to move to the United States: It has areas with warm weather in winter, areas with low living costs, great sports, culture, cuisine, libraries—the list is almost endless. But there are potential problems that must be recognized and avoided. With its combination of federal, state, and local income taxes, the United States presents tax planning issues that make Canadian tax compliance seem a trifle. The cost of obeying all of this law measured in time, professional fees, and eventual taxes can be immense.

The United States is far and away the top choice of Canadians who want familiar surroundings, familiar customs, and warmer weather. Some states offer lower taxes and lower living costs than many regions of Canada. But problems arise at the border with new, stiff requirements that Canadians going to the United States have passports. For short stays, U.S. immigration rules are not burdensome for Canadians. For stays of more than 183 days in each calendar year and for anyone who purchases land or property in the United States, tax reporting issues arise. Unless these issues are dealt with fully and directly, American tax and border authorities can turn what was intended to be a pleasant retirement into an object lesson on tax enforcement. The United States floats on a sea of litigation. Only the foolish ignore the risks of winding up in civil or even criminal prosecutions for conduct, including minor stock trading compliance issues and product labelling matters, that would be worthy of no more than a polite reminder from a Canadian regulatory authority. The American approach is formal to a fault. Foretold is forewarned.

Income tax issues have been anticipated by both governments. Canada and the United States have a treaty that eliminates most of the worries about being taxed twice on income, but the treaty does not eliminate all problems. It is often thought that U.S. income taxes are lower than Canada's. It's true in the sense that high-income earners may pay lower rates in some tax brackets and that high Canadian tax brackets hit incomes at lower levels than U.S. high brackets. But when you add in state and local income taxes, user fees for things that are part of government services in Canada, and the high cost of medical care and medical insurance in the United States, much of the tax "gap" is eliminated or even reversed. Moreover, for those U.S. taxpayers subjects to the Alternative Minimum Tax, all bets are off. These folks can pay taxes far above the standard U.S. income tax rates.

"Whether one pays lower income taxes in the U.S. than in Canada depends on the places you compare," says Caroline Nalbantoglu, a Registered Financial Planner with PWL Advisors Inc. in Montreal. "Don't forget that there are U.S. estate taxes, Social Security taxes that are much higher than Canadian Pension Plan levies, more user fees for things that are covered by government in Canada, state and local income taxes. When you add it up, the idea that U.S. taxes are lower than those in Canada is erroneous. Only in a few jurisdictions like Nevada, where there are neither state income tax nor sales taxes, the bite is less."

Spending more than half the year in the United States or having a green card will make you a U.S. resident for tax purposes and open up a Pandora's box of complexities. If you are considered to be a U.S. resident under the physical presence test of spending more than 183 days in the United States, you can still be treated as a non-resident for U.S. tax purposes if your life as demonstrated by the location of your home, family, and source of income is still principally in Canada. The U.S. Internal Revenue Service has Form 8840 for this purpose. It has to be filed by June 15 of the year following the year for which you are seeking an exemption from U.S. taxes.

It has been said that when you double your exposure to national tax systems, you increase your reporting burdens by a factor of ten. The Canada–U.S. Tax Treaty is supposed to reduce the risks of double taxation, but it does this only at a high cost of sweat, bookkeeping, and professional guidance. Note that the Tax Treaty does not necessarily provide relief from state income taxes in the United States.

Living in the United States exposes you to the possibility of having your estate become vulnerable to American death duties. They can be avoided by such measures as having real estate held in trusts that carry on regardless of death. Those exposed to American estate taxes can make gifts within annual limits to reduce tax exposure. Anyone exposed to U.S. income or succession duties should consult counsel familiar with cross-border taxation. The fees spent for advice will be money well invested.

For an excellent treatment of tax consequences for Canadians considering residency in the United States, see KPMG, *Tax Planning 2008 for You and Your Family* (Toronto: Carswell, 2007), pp. 271–86. The guide is revised annually.

Tax Havens

Jurisdictions that do not have income taxes or that have very low income taxes often beckon. Promoters pitch these places, pointing out that you can save a great deal by not having to cough up 25 to 45 percent of your income to Ottawa and the provinces.

There is, however, a relationship between tax rates and quality of government. It is not perfectly proportional, but high taxes in Scandinavia averaging 50 percent of national Gross Domestic Product do buy huge amounts of cradle-to-grave social services.

Rates are lower in the U.K., New Zealand, and Germany, averaging 30 to 36 percent of national GDP and, in turn, people in those countries get less government service than Scandinavians. Tax rates are still lower in the United States at 26 percent of GDP although the poor are worse off than they are in the mid-range or upper range of tax-ranked jurisdictions.[2]

Tax havens—the run-of-the-mill jurisdictions like Vanuatu, Nauru, and Tonga in the South Seas; Oman in the Middle East; Monaco in Europe; the Caymans and the Turks and Caicos in the Caribbean—are variously remote from much of the rest of the world or very costly. Nauru is famously xenophobic and, in any case, has been mined for fertilizer so that its deeply cratered land resembles a lunar landscape. Monaco is so expensive that only major rock stars and entrepreneurs with over-the-top fortunes can afford the place. And Dubai, a nice spot in the Middle East, is costly but not quite a watering spot for North Americans. Pleasantly mild in winter, the heat rises to astonishing levels in summer to as much as 45 degrees Celsius, which is enough to cook a chicken slowly.

Tax Logic

In the end, a tax haven is about personal circumstance as much as it is about fissures in international tax agreements. For example, Canada, which taxes only accrued but unrealized capital gains at death, seems a tax haven for wealthy Americans who face succession duties on the entirety of their estates—subject to reforms of inheritance tax law.

Finally, a word of caution. Tax authorities in countries with progressive income taxes tend to be harsh when they find that a person they would like to tax has made that difficult. If you plan to stay in Canada or to live in the United States, it could be best to skip the idea of a haven and just pay up. Flight to avoid taxation, even if done in a way compliant with Canadian law and after payment of Canadian departure taxes, can involve long-term separation from family and friends. It can be a very costly way to retire.

Chapter Summary

Life away from Canada has obvious charms, based on weather most of the time but also lower taxes or perhaps just the lure of something different. Before immigrating to another land, check the costs very carefully, estimate what it will cost to pay the Canadian departure tax on accrued but unrealized capital gains, and what medical and hospital insurance, housing, transportation, etc., will cost. The dollars and cents need to add up.

Chapter 11

The Future of Retirement

Retirement, as we know it, a right backed by government funding, is a comparatively recent concept and it may not last. Retirement became social policy and a popular expectation in late 19th century Germany and spread to Europe and across the Atlantic to Canada after World War I.

Three important trends were at work in building retirement as a national policy in the nations that adopted it. First, there had to be an economic surplus. Subsistence farming cannot generate that surplus, but huge increases in industrial production in the 19th century allowed nations to build enough wealth to support people who don't work. Second, there had to be a rapidly growing labour force to replace retiring workers and to generate income that could be transferred to older workers. Third, there had to be a social catalyst to combine these two forces. In 19th-century Germany, Chancellor Otto von Bismarck used the concept of retirement to co-opt social reformers and to embed the idea that a rich empire would take care of its workers. It was a way to take the fire from early socialist movements that made retirement part of their pitch to potential members. In North America and Britain and in much of Europe, organized labour took the lead in demanding retirement programs. Unions, which grew in importance and influence around the world in the 1920s and 1930s, favoured national pension schemes. Such plans were good for their members and were a way to get older workers out of the labour force to make way for younger workers.

After World War II, with spreading affluence and millions of young soldiers leaving the armed services, it was vital to open up jobs. Rosie the Riveter, the industrial version of Betty Crocker, had replaced men in the labour force during the war. She went back to her kitchen, and her job was taken over by the ex-soldiers. Retirement at ages specified in union-management contracts, supported by organized labour, enforced in law, financed by the spread of defined benefit pension plans with accompanying tax benefits for employers, and accepted by society, became the norm.

Governments in Canada and the United States wanted to reduce the risk that an army of the unemployed would topple them. There had been such armies—or, if you prefer, mobs—in Britain after World War I. Canada had the Winnipeg General Strike in 1919. The United States had a more insidious vigilante movement designed to block the ascent of Afro-Americans. In the American south, guerilla goon squads dressed in white sheets forced African-American citizens to remain share croppers and blocked their economic ascent through better-paying jobs. We cannot forget Germany, where the unemployed were early backers of National Socialism in some cases and Soviet-style communism in others. Compulsory retirement was an expense for government, but it was a way to offer jobs to people who might otherwise seek radical changes of government. It was sold as a benevolent social policy to older workers who were put out to pasture.

Today, retirement operates in a vastly different economic environment. Nations and individuals in the advanced economies of Canada, the United States, and the European Union certainly have the means to produce an economic surplus that can be transferred or retained by older workers. But the labour forces of Canada, Italy, and other EU nations are stable or shrinking. The pressure to force people to retire from the labour force is off.

Over the next 35 years, baby boomers born as late as 1960 will be moving from young old age—the years from 65 to 75—to middle old age—the years from 75 to 85. Birth rates in Canada and other advanced countries are falling. The result is that Canada's population of people over age 65 will double by 2030. By that year, the percentage of the elderly in Canada's population will be 40 percent compared to 52 percent for Japan, 48 percent for Italy, 47 percent for Germany, 40 percent for France, and 31 percent for the United States. By 2050, Canada will have 44 percent of its population over 65 compared to 72 percent for Japan, 68 percent for Italy, 50 percent for Germany, 46 percent for France, and 32 percent for the United States.[1] These nations will have to retain older workers at their jobs or face devastating economic contraction.

Older workers who pay taxes will be able to pay for some of their medical benefits for, as tax-paying employees, they help finance their own pills and operations. As the proportion of the elderly in a population rises, nations find it harder to finance their medical needs and retirements. Pension plans have to rely on pay-as-you-go funding through which younger workers pay for older workers' benefits. To relieve the tax burden on younger workers, national pension authorities take steps to discourage early retirement. As we've seen, the Canada and Quebec Pension Plans penalize members for taking early retirement by providing a smaller pension payment to those who opt to take it before 65 and rewarding those who put off receiving it until some time after 65.

The recent trend to retire early appears headed for its own demise. Demography will force an extension of work years, ending the trend to declining work years and expanding retirement years. The trend to amend laws that force people out of the labour force will result in longer working lives. We can be sure that by 2028, the average age of workers in the labour force will be higher than it currently is.[2]

There will be an irony in the phenomenon of the greying of the labour force. Seniors will be more able to afford to retire. But they will balance the incentives to keep working with the income from not working. We can predict that the incentives to stay on the job will grow and that average incomes will tend to rise rather than plateauing or declining with age, as they do now.

Postponement of retirement by 10 or 20 years has large financial advantages. People on the track to retirement may be able to continue to contribute to retirement plans and to grow their non-registered savings. If they can manage a 7 percent nominal return on assets, they will be able to double their invested money in a decade. It may be objected that this is foolishness and that pushing back the end of work just means that wealthier people will have less time to enjoy what they have built.

QUESTION: What demographic force will work to end compulsory retirement at set ages?

ANSWER: A lower birth rate, fewer younger workers, and a need to retain older workers in the labour force.

Perhaps. But it will be a voluntary process, not one that is enforced. And that voluntariness is consistent with the ideals of a society in which age is not a basis for discrimination. To those who say that it is irrational to labour for another decade in late life, only to have fewer years, there is an answer: Take more vacations, go upmarket with the income that comes from working longer, or go on adventure travel junkets. It is a matter of taste, of course. The point is that money creates choice. People facing retirement deserve the right to choose.

Topping the Parabola

A declining birth rate in most of Europe and much of the rest of the developed world combined with growing exclusionism in immigration policy will force changes in social policy to maintain the employability of older workers. We may expect that the ending of compulsory retirement will be followed by tax changes that increase the ability of older workers to retain employment income, that provide favourable tax treatment for bonuses received after age 65, and that link tax credits to continued employment. The federal government has already moved the termination date for individual RRSP contributions from 69 to 71 and added a new tax shelter that can extend tax-free accumulation after age 71, the Tax-Free Savings Account. The trend of tax law is clearly toward encouraging or at least not discouraging remaining in the labour force late in life. The TFSA gives no tax deduction for money coming in but allows growth within the plan without tax and payouts without tax and with no restrictions on amounts that are withdrawn.

As nations revert to policies that will sustain employment of older workers, the cost of whether to continue to work or leave it will become clearer. We can expect that more incentives to continue work will result in an increase in the participation rate of persons over 65 in gainful employment.

That employment will, however, be a matter of style. The conventional model of full-time employment will have to give way to combinations of part-time employment with extended vacations. After all, the labour force has made accommodation for women who want to take extended leaves for child bearing and rearing. The Canada Pension Plan has found ways to compensate women for time out for their maternal work. It will be easier to accommodate a model in which full-time employees evolve into part-time workers.

Employment law and pension administration can make the changes. But there will remain critical economic issues that the employed or those who wish to be employed will have to make for themselves.

It will be easier to keep a job with good wages and benefits or a very good salary than to find one. Income rises with education and training. Employers cannot be expected to invest the same amount of education and training in newly hired old employees than in newly hired young ones. The payback period for older employees is less than for younger employees. Reduced job mobility among older employees may reduce the payback period bias that works in favour of the young, but it is unlikely to eliminate it altogether. Starting over at 65 is going to remain a tougher process than staying employed at age 65.

Health costs rise with age. The longer people work, the more of these costs they can finance. Employers can bear the costs of supplemental health care plans, average them out across all employees—clearly a move that harms the interests of the young, healthy employee—or, alternatively, reduce benefits, increase deductibles for employees, or get government subsidies for keeping on older workers. Subsidies ultimately raise costs. They discriminate against the majority in favour of a minority. They can misallocate resources and have political implications that could haunt the parties that impose them. The solution, of course, is to allow older people to continue to work in order to finance their own health benefits.

There are, in the end, some facts of economics that governments cannot change. For example, women have longer life expectancies than men and therefore receive lower payments from annuities at any age. By way of balance, women pay lower life insurance premiums for coverage equal to that for a man.

The best regulatory framework for the extension of work into years beyond what is not conventional retirement is likely to be the one with the fewest rules and the lowest costs. It may seem anachronistic to say it, but the market may be the best allocation mechanism for human capital. Let the elderly show what they can do. They have low job mobility in comparison to the high job mobility of young workers and they have experience.

Starting at Sixty-five

The job market will not turn employment into a late-life utopia. The reality is that for those who would like to work beyond 65, it is going to be useful either to stay on the job or at least to find jobs or companies in which there can be a direct transfer of experience from work at an earlier age. Remaining employed or in the same field overcomes the argument that it costs too much to train an older worker. Staying put makes it relatively easy to do part-time work in a familiar setting. And staying put avoids the challenges or misgiving of taking jobs with lower pay or prestige than the ones given up at formal retirement.

It has been a truism that income declines with age. The departure from formal or customary work to the extended leisure of retirement has been an explanation for why seniors have lower incomes than people in the middle years of life. Yet asset ownership tends to rise with age. By age 60 or 65, most mortgages are paid and people are reaching their highest levels of asset ownership. These two facts together can argue for living off investments and reducing work. The benefit of this plan may be lower tax bills and perhaps a higher level of disposable investment income. The flaw in the argument is that there will be at least 60 to 70 percent of employment income left after tax, the exact amount depending on the province of residence.

The arguments for and against retirement have to confront the reality that leaving formal work tends to be a one-way journey. You can start a second career at age 55 or 60 or 70. But that may mean starting over as an hourly employee in a service business. That is not an attractive extension of work for many people.

Contemplating retirement today means accepting that reality. That reality argues strongly for thinking retirement through with great care. Work and career are perhaps metaphors for life itself. Retirement well earned is a celebration. But retirement accepted without planning is perilous. Retire if you will or if you must, but do it with open eyes and a sharp pencil. Coming down the mountain is a lot easier than climbing back up.

Chapter Summary

Compulsory retirement grew as a social policy as a way of getting younger workers into the labour force. The expense of this move was borne by older workers who tended to accept old age unemployment in exchange for pension schemes underwritten by government or financed by government via tax benefits for companies that had retirement plans. Lower birth rates in developed countries will tend to end compulsory retirement. As well, high training costs for new employees will motivate companies to keep productive older workers. Finally, having older workers remain on the job to generate savings for their own pensions and to transfer income to pay for their health care makes financial sense for government.

Glossary

I have listed terms and phrases in the book so that readers can have
a ready explanation for them. As well, I have included some terms
that are part of pension literature for readers who want to pursue
topics beyond *When Can I Retire?*

Actuarial Valuation
A mathematical analysis of the financial status of a pension plan.
Following the analysis, the managing board of the plan may raise
or lower contribution rates so that the inflow of funds meets the
liabilities of the plan.

Actuary
A person who is a Fellow of the Canadian Institute of Actuaries.

Allocation
In the pension context, the designation of pension benefits to one
or more beneficiaries.

Annuity
An insurance contract that sets a sum of money to be paid period-
ically out of a capital sum for the life of the recipient, called the
annuitant, or for the life of the annuitant and another person,
usually the spouse. The payments may be for a life, the last of two
lives, and for a minimum number of years.

Beneficiary

Person(s) designated to receive either a benefit from a pension plan, an insurance contract, or a residual interest in an estate. If a beneficiary is not named, then by law the decedent's estate becomes the beneficiary and funds remaining after payment of debts may be distributed according to the rules of intestacy of the applicable jurisdiction.

Benefit Formula

A provision in a pension plan for calculating a member's defined benefit according to years of service and career or final average to find a fixed dollar amount or a flat benefit rate of payment.

Best Five-Year Average

A benefit formula for calculating a member's benefit by applying the member's average earnings during the five years when earnings were at their highest level.

Bond

A promissory note issued by a company or government, Crown corporation, or supranational authority (such as the World Bank). Bonds may have fixed coupons or changeable interest rates and have fixed terms when due or no terms in the case of perpetual bonds, which have, in the past, also been called consols.

Bridging

A temporary benefit provided to members of a pension plan who retire prior to the age when CPP/QPP benefits are normally payable, i.e., at age 65 in order to supplement the pension until the CPP/QPP benefits began to flow.

Canada Pension Plan (CPP)

A federal pension plan with death, disability, and survivor benefits. Administered by Human Resources Development Canada, it operates in all provinces and territories except Quebec, which has a nearly identical Quebec Pension Plan (QPP). CPP beneficiaries may begin taking benefits at age 60. That triggers a reduction equal to $^1/_2$ of 1 percent per month for each month prior to age 65 that benefits begin. Beneficiaries who delay taking benefits may wait as long as age 70. For each month after age 65 that benefits begin, the beneficiary receives $^1/_2$ of 1 percent of the age 65 monthly benefit as a bonus. CPP benefits are indexed to the cost of living.

Career Average Plan

A defined benefit plan that applies the unit of benefit to earnings of the member in each year of service and not to the final or final average earnings.

Closed-End Fund

An asset pool that is held by a trustee for the benefit of investors in the fund. Unlike a mutual fund, which values assets daily and sells and redeems units at net asset value, the closed-end fund neither sells nor redeems, but allows investors to trade shares on the market much like the shares of other corporations.

Commuted Value

The amount of money paid or payable in a one-time payment that is equal in value to the sum of future pension benefits. Employees are entitled to receive the commuted value of their pensions if they leave a pension plan and if the contributions have vested, that is, become theirs.

Contributory Plan

A pension plan that requires employees to make contributions by payroll deduction in order to qualify for benefits under the plan.

Debenture

A promissory note, usually a bond, that is backed by the general credit and assets of the issuing company rather than by specific, defined assets.

Deferred Profit-Sharing Plan

A plan that allows an employer to contribute regularly each year or irregularly in various years sums that may be invested in the employer's shares. A retiring employee may remove money as a lump sum but must be paid out no later than 90 days after termination of employment. DPSP payouts may be staggered over as much as a decade.

Defined Benefit Plan

A pension plan that defines the pension to be provided based on earnings but not total contributions. If the plan is contributory, the rate of employee contributions may be specified in the plan with the employer paying the balance of costs.

Defined Contribution Plan

A plan that sets benefits based on accumulated contributions of employer and employee and the return on the investment of the funds contributed.

Dollar Cost Averaging

A method of reducing risk by spreading the amount contributed to a pension plan or RRSP over time. If a constant sum is contributed over every period, then when asset prices are low, you get more shares or units of an asset; when asset prices are high, you wind up with fewer shares or units.

Duration

A measure of the sensitivity of a bond to changes in prevailing interest rates. Expressed in years, duration shows the weighted average time for an investor to realize the currently stated yield to maturity of the fund.

Expense Ratio

The proportion of costs, including management fees and trading and overhead costs, and operating expenses per unit of a fund divided by the net asset value per unit of the fund.

Fully Funded

The condition of a pension plan when it has sufficient assets to meet its actuarially determined obligations.

Funding

Systematic payments, usually monthly, into pension funds that, along with investment returns on funds invested, are intended to provide benefits as they become payable.

GARP

Growth at a Reasonable Price is a method of valuing growth stocks with a constraint imposed by the ratio of share price to earnings per share. See PEG ratio.

Growth Stock

A share of a corporation that is estimated to grow in intrinsic value, usually expressed as earnings per share, at a rate faster than that of the market on which it is traded.

G-RRSP

A group RRSP.

Guaranteed Income Supplement (GIS)

A system that pays OAS recipients additional income if they fall below given income guidelines.

Hedge Fund

A mutual-type fund that engages in short selling as well as conventional purchases of stocks or bonds. Hedge funds may borrow and so "leverage" their assets. Hedge funds typically have higher fees than mutual funds and may have more widely scattered returns. Some hedge funds impose minimum holding periods of one, two, three, or more years on their investors.

Index Fund

A portfolio of stocks or bonds that replicates a major index such as the Standard & Poor's 500 Composite or the S&P/TSX Total Return Index. There is no active management and management fees, as a result, are typically much lower than fees for actively managed funds. Sometimes called passively managed funds.

Indexing

A provision in a pension plan that requires periodic adjustments to benefits after retirement to compensate for changes in the cost of living.

Investment Advisors
Persons or companies hired to select stocks, bonds, real estate, or other assets for investment by pension plans.

Investment Return
Earnings of a pension fund from stocks, bonds, property, or other assets.

Joint and Survivor Pension or Annuity
An annuity payable until the death of the later of the employee or his or her spouse.

LIF (Life Income Fund)
A variation on the Registered Retirement Income Fund in which the beneficiary has control of investments, but is limited in the amounts that can be taken out each year. LIF rules require the beneficiary to buy an annuity with any residual funds at age 80.

LIRA (Locked-In Retirement Account)
An RRSP that is intended to be used to provide a pension.

LRIF (Locked-In Retirement Income Fund)
Similar to a LIF with caps on amounts that can be taken out each year but without the LIF's requirement to buy an annuity at age 80.

Locking In
Barriers to withdrawal from designated plans to ensure that beneficiaries do not deplete plan assets too quickly.

Managed Fund

A mutual fund that employs a manager to pick stocks or other assets. Sometimes called actively managed fund. Fees tend to be appreciably higher than those for index funds.

Money Purchase Plan

Another name for a defined contribution plan.

Multi-employer Pension Plan (MEP)

A multi-employer plan is one in which no more than 95 percent of active members will be employed by one employer or group of employers in the year.

Mutual Fund

An investment fund that is valued, usually at the end of every trading day, and into which investors may put money at the fund's net asset value at the close of each trading day. Investors may redeem units at the price of units at the end of each trading day. See closed-end fund.

OAS (Old Age Security)

The basic federal pension plan for people age 65 or older who meet various criteria for residence in Canada.

Past Service Pension Adjustment

If an employer improves a pension plan or if an employee wishes to generate pension credits for time he or she was not in a plan, it is possible to add to the pension base via what is often called a "buy back," which adds to what the plan will eventually pay; this process is known as the Past Service Pension Adjustment (PSPA). Ironically, if the PSPA increases the value of the plan, the Pension

Adjustment (see below) may retroactively decrease past RRSP contribution room. Then a carryforward RRSP withdrawal tax liability will exist that can be used up in future RRSP contribution room or, if in excess of that tax-free room, will result in a tax liability.

PEG Ratio

A measure of stock performance in which the share price divided by earnings per share is divided by the growth rate of earnings per share. See GARP.

Pension

A fixed amount of money paid on a regular periodic basis to a person or surviving dependent in recognition of previous employment or service.

Pension Adjustment (PA)

The value of pension contributions generated in a prior year. The adjustment reduces the limit of what you can contribute to the RRSP. Pension sources that generate the PA include Deferred Profit-Sharing Plans, Defined Contribution Pension Plans, and Defined Benefit Contribution Pension Plans. People who have no employer-sponsored pension plan have no PA limit or deduction on their annual RRSP contribution limit.

Pension Adjustment Reversal (PAR)

When a beneficiary leaves a Registered Pension Plan or a Deferred Profit-Sharing Plan before retirement, the PAR increases the limit to which a person can add funds to his or her RRSP. PARs are issued when people leave an employer for a new job or if a Defined Benefit Pension Plan terminates.

Pensioner

One who is receiving a pension from a pension plan.

Pension Plan

A program established by an employer, union, or other member-based labour organization to provide benefits to an employee or member when that person retires.

Pension Portability

A rule that allows pension credits or accrued benefits to be switched from one employer's plan to another. See Reciprocal Agreement.

Quebec Pension Plan (QPP)

Established in 1966, the QPP has the same rate of contributions, year's maximum pensionable earnings, and annual indexation as the Canada Pension Plan. Certain ancillary benefits vary from those provided by the CPP.

Real Rate of Return

The after-inflation return of any investment process.

Real Return Bond

A bond issued typically by a government that pays a rate of return adjusted to maintain purchasing power as defined by changes in a relevant cost of living index.

Reciprocal Agreement

An agreement negotiated with another pension plan that allows members to transfer their pensions when they switch employers or plans.

Registered Retirement Income Fund (RRIF)

A prescribed retirement income payment plan that allows for payout of funds within an RRSP. There are no caps on payouts, but there are annual minima that must be taken out.

Registered Retirement Saving Plan (RRSP)

A personal retirement savings plan defined by Canada's Income Tax Act. Sums contributed within prescribed limits in the year of contribution or the following 60 days are eligible for deduction from earned income.

Retiring Allowance

Defined by the Income Tax Act as a payment made on or after retirement in consequence of a number of years of service or in respect of loss of employment. Within defined limits, retiring allowances, seen as deferred wages or salaries, may be transferred tax-free to an RRSP.

Segregated Fund

A stock or bond portfolio with a guarantee of 80 percent or 100 percent of return of at least the cost of investment after a hold period of 5 but more commonly 10 years. Seg funds typically add an insurance charge to the underlying mutual fund fee.

Surplus

A surplus arises when pension fund actuaries determine that a pension plan has more assets than are needed to satisfy the estimated liabilities of the fund.

Value Stock

A share of a company that is thought to be trading for less than its intrinsic value as reflected by such ratios as share prices to earnings per share. Stocks with p/e ratios below market or industry averages are often considered to be value stocks.

Vesting
The process by which the employer's contribution to an employee's pension becomes the property of that employee. When vesting does occur, the employee is entitled to the commuted value of the pension should he or she leave the employer.

YMPE
The Year's Maximum Pensionable Earnings is a Canada Pension Plan/Quebec Pension Plan measure that sets a maximum amount of earnings on which one is required to contribute to the plan. The YMPE for 2008 is $44,900.

Further Reading

Andrew Allentuck, *Bonds for Canadians: How to Build Wealth and Lower Risk in Your Portfolio* (Toronto: John Wiley & Sons, 2006). Bonds tend to soar when stocks are sinking. This book explains how to invest for safety as well as profit.

William Bernstein, *The Intelligent Asset Allocator* (New York: McGraw-Hill, 2001). This distinguished financial analyst, who is also a neurologist, offers guidance to asset allocation and the use of index funds.

David Bogan and Keith Davies, *Avoid Retirement and Stay Alive: The New Retirement Revolution* (New York: McGraw-Hill, 2008). The case against retirement in a U.S. setting.

Bruce Cohen and Brian FitzGerald, *The Pension Puzzle* (3d ed.; Toronto: John Wiley & Sons, 2007). An excellent guide to pensions and government benefits by a fine personal finance writer (Cohen) and an actuary (FitzGerald).

Sherry Cooper, *The New Retirement: How It Will Change Our Future* (Toronto: Viking Canada, 2008). A bank economist discusses the economic framework of retirement.

Tamara Erickson, *Retire Retirement* (Cambridge, Mass.: Harvard Business Press, 2008). Erickson argues that older workers are often more productive and profitable than their younger colleagues and that older persons form markets that are increasingly attractive. Context is U.S. and international.

Douglas Gray, *The Canadian Snowbird Guide: What You Need to Know about Living Part-Time in the USA and Mexico* (4th ed.; Toronto: John Wiley & Sons, 2008). A popular guide for Canadians who want to spend some time in these countries.

James O'Shaughnessy, *How to Retire Rich: Time-Tested Strategies to Beat the Market and Retire in Style* (New York: Broadway Books, 1998). A review and analysis of investment strategies.

Gordon Pape, *The Retirement Time Bomb: How to Achieve Financial Independence in a Changing World* (Toronto: Penguin, 2006). A distinguished financial author discusses investment strategies.

Paul Petillo, *Retirement Planning for the Utterly Confused* (New York: McGraw-Hill, 2008). Investment strategies in a U.S. context.

Jeremy J. Siegel, *The Future for Investors* (New York: Crown Business, 2005). A highly respected economist who teaches at the Wharton School of the University of Pennsylvania provides a framework for picking stocks likely to do well in the long run.

Notes

Chapter 1: Retirement: The Destination and the Trouble of Getting There

1. Associated Press, April 26, 2007, per MSNBC.com.

2. Statistics Canada, The Daily, March 14, 2001.

3. See Canadian Institute of Actuaries, Canada News Wire, June 12, 2007, re "Planning for Retirement: Are Canadians Saving Enough?"

4. Associated Press, March 12, 2007, MSNBC.com.

5. Canada, Department of Finance, Budget, 2005, Annex 3.

6. Anne Howland, "Early Retirement Payoff Must End," *National Post*, July 4, 2007, p. FP 14.

7. Senate Standing Committee on Banking, Trade and Commerce, *The Demographic Time Bomb: Mitigating the Effects of Demographic Change in Canada*, June 2006; see http://www.parl.gc.ca/39/1/parlbus/commbus/senate/com-e/bank-e/rep-e/rep03jun06-e.htm.

8. Montreal Economic Institute, "The Retirement Age in Quebec: A Worrying Situation," *Economic Note*, June 2007, p. 1.

9. Ibid., pp. 2–3.

10. See Sherry Cooper, *The New Retirement* (Toronto: Viking Canada, 2008), pp. 74–81.

11. Jeremy J. Siegel, *Stocks for the Long Run* (3d ed.; New York: McGraw-Hill, 2002), p. 13.

12. An economist might ask if the effort of study will produce increasing or decreasing returns. Chances are that starting from scratch, the returns to study will increase rapidly. The saturation point in knowledge surely exists, but it is at some level of information that has probably never been reached.

Chapter 2: The Big Gamble: Setting Up a Retirement Plan

1. See Michael Decter and Francesca Grosso, *Navigating Canada's Health Care: A User Guide to Getting the Care You Need* (Toronto:

Penguin, 2007). See especially Chapter 10, "Navigating Health Care for Seniors."

2. Statistics Canada, Census, 2006: Portrait of the Canadian Population in 2006 by Age and Sex, July 17, 2007.

3. Gordon Pape, *The Retirement Time Bomb* (Toronto: Penguin, 2006), p. 56.

4. See Social Security Administration, Period Life Table at http://www.ssa.gov/OACT/STATS/table4c6.html. For an interesting comparison to health-adjusted life expectancies by gender and Canadian province, see Statistics Canada data at http://www40.statcan.ca/l01/cst01/hlth67.htm.

Chapter 3: The Decision Point

1. "Retirement: A New Life after Work?" *AXA Retirement Scope*, January 2005. See http://www.retirement-scope.axa.com/lib/rs/uploads2/ameriques/canada/AXA_Report_2005_canada_en.pdf.

2. Sherry Cooper, *The New Retirement* (Toronto: Viking Canada, 2008), p. 7.

3. Ibid. And see Gary Burtless and Joseph F. Quinn, "Retirement Trends and Policies to Encourage Work Among Older Americans," Brookings Institution, January 2000.

4. Sally K. Rigler, "Alcoholism in the Elderly," *American Family Physician*, March 15, 2000.

5. Max L. Stek et al., "Is Depression in Old Age Fatal Only When People Feel Lonely?" *American Journal of Psychiatry*, January 2005, pp. 178ff.

Chapter 4: Budgeting for the Future

1. See http://www.bankofcanada.ca/en/backgrounders/bg-i4.html for an explanation of CPI construction and categories.

2. Bruce Cohen and Brian FitzGerald, *The Pension Puzzle* (3d ed.; Toronto: John Wiley & Sons, 2007) p. 5.

3. It is helpful to distinguish wealth from income. Wealth as a term refers to capital. Income is just that. One may be wealthy with little income; those who keep their money in art on the walls or in jewellery in vaults are in such a position. Those with high incomes may spend what they earn and wind up with little or no wealth.

4. See http://naturalmedicine.suite101.com/article.cfm/depression_ and_food.

5. See http://www.edmuncs.com/new/2007/honda/accord/100782896/ cto.html?.

6. See also http://www.howlandtax.com/articles/cars.htm.

7. For a critical illness coverage calculator, see http://www. manulife.ca/canada/Canada1.nsf/Public/CI_Calculator.

8. See Michael Decter and Francesca Grosso, *Navigating Canada's Health Care: A User Guide to Getting the Care You Need* (Toronto: Penguin, 2006).

9. See Appendix to V. Demers et al., "Comparison of Provincial Prescription Drug Plans and the Impact on Patients' Annual Drug Expenditures," *Canadian Medical Association Journal*, February 12, 2008, pp. 405–409.

Chapter 5: Where Will the Money Come From? Public Pensions

1. The Fidelity study is not quite disinterested. Fidelity sells its products through certain financial planners who receive commissions and yearly fees for Fidelity products that are kept in client accounts. Not surprisingly, Fidelity suggests that people thinking about retirement or planning it "seek professional advice." Not a bad idea, but professional advice varies in its quality. Fidelity's survey shows, it says, that the replacement rate of income in retirement rises in the presence of advisors. The relationship, however, is far from certain. Advisors prefer clients with lots of money that can generate lots of commissions. Hence one could say that the replacement rate rises with income. See Fidelity Investments Canada, *The Changing State of Retirement in Canada*, at http://www.fidelity.ca/takethechallenge.

Chapter 6: Where Will the Money Come From? Employment and Private Pension Sources

1. See Christine Wiedman and Heather Wier, "Defined-Benefit Pension Plans: The Staying Power of Deficits," *Ivey Business Journal*, September/October 2005, available online at http://www. iveybusinessjournal.com/view_article.asp?intArticle_ID=580.

2. See Janet White, "Eaton's Lost Ones," *Benefits Canada*, December 1999.

3. Grant Surridge, "Funding Levels out of Crisis," *National Post*, July 10, 2007, p. FP1.

4. Bruce Cohen and Brian FitzGerald, *The Pension Puzzle* (3d ed.; Toronto: John Wiley & Sons, 2007), p. 81.

5. For more information on rising RRSP limits, see KPMG, *Tax Planning 2008* (Toronto: Thomson Carswell, 2007), p. 39.

6. See KPMG, *Tax Planning for You and Your Family 2008* (Toronto: Thomson Carswell, 2007), pp. 40–41.

7. Ibid., see p. 296.

8. See Case Study: "Confederation Life Insurance Co.," Sungard Bancware ERISK, 2007.

9. Qualifying pension income does not include Canada Pension Plan benefits, Old Age Security payments, or Guaranteed Income Supplement benefits. It really means private pension income received through a life annuity. If the beneficiary is 65 or over and receiving payments as a result of the death of a spouse, it also includes annuities from an RRSP or deferred profit-sharing plan, a payment out of a RRIF, or the income portion of a conventional annuity.

10. See http://www.fsco.gov.on.ca/english/PENSIONS/newunlocking forms-2006.asp.

11. See Government of Canada, Department of Finance, "Improvements to Life Income Funds Give Canadians More Flexibility," May 8, 2008; see http://www.fin.gc.ca/news08/08-037e.html. See also comments of Jamie Golombek, "Busy Summer for Tax Planning," *National Post*, July 26, 2008, p. FW5.

12. http://www.budget.gc.ca/2008/pamphlet-depliant/pamphlet-depliant2-eng.asp.

13. Tim Cestnick, "The New Tax-Free Savings Account: Does It Replace Your RRSP?" *Globe and Mail*, February 28, 2008, p. B-19.

Chapter 7: Managing Retirement Assets

1. Aswath Damodaran, *Investment Philosophies* (New York: John Wiley & Sons, 2003), p. 289.

2. Ibid., pp. 296–99.

3. Rob Carrick, "Head to Head, Pros Trample the Ordinary Joes," Globe and Mail, January 5, 2008, p. B14.

4. Bloomberg Business News, *Globe and Mail*, January 3, 2008, p. B8.

5. See William Bernstein, *The Intelligent Asset Allocator* (New York: McGraw-Hill, 2001), Chapter 8. You can employ the same buy-low, sell-high strategy with managed mutual funds, but sales loads of up to 6 percent and backload penalties imposed by some funds can make this strategy costly. The strategy clearly works best with index funds. See also Bernstein's *The Four Pillars of Investing* (New York: McGraw-Hill, 2002), Chapters 13 and 14.

6. See Moshe Milevsky, *Money Logic: Financial Strategies for the Smart Investor* (Toronto: Stoddart, 1989), pp. 49–70.

7. Jonathan Chevreau, "Insurer Jumps on Fund Wagon," *National Post*, October 5, 2006, pp. 10–11.

8. See Rob Carrick, "Costly Protection for the Retiring Type," *Globe and Mail*, March 9, 2008, p. B-18.

9. Interview with Jason Agaby, vice-president for product development, Dynamic Funds, July 9, 2008.

10. Ibid.

11. Wendy Cuthbert, "Reverse Mortgage Marketplace Heats Up," *Investment Executive*, October 2007, p. 36.

12. Darcy Keith, "Reverse Loan May Be Forward Thinking," *National Post*, April 3, 2008, pp. SR1, SR4.

13. Cuthbert, p. 36.

14. Keith, p. SR4.

15. Colin Perkel, "Many Canadians Facing Bleak Retirement Years," *Winnipeg Free Press*, June 15, 2007, p. A15.

16. Roma Luciw, "Retire? For Some Boomers It's Death Do Them Part," *Globe and Mail*, October 19, 2007, pp. C1–C2.

17. Canadian Centre for Elder Law Studies, Study Paper on Viatical Settlements (Vancouver, B.C.: The Law Foundation of British Columbia), CCELS Report No. 3, BCLI report No. 43, May 2006, p. iii.

18. Ibid., p. 7.

19. Ibid., p. 26.

Chapter 8: What Are You Going to Do with All Those Years?

1. "Retiring Mandatory Retirement," CBC News, December 12, 2006.

2. Human Resources and Social Development Canada, "Mandatory Retirement in Canada," January 4, 2007.

3. Janice Tibbetts, "Top Court Rejects Man's Mandatory Retirement Case," *National Post,* July 19, 2008, p. A5.

4. American Psychological Association Online. See http://www. psychologymatters.org/retirement.html.

5. See http://www.frenchentree.com/fe-legal/DisplayArticle.asp? ID=2173.

6. Bonnie Rothman Morris, "When Retirement Leaves an Emptiness, Some Fill It with Alcohol," *New York Times,* May 18, 2004.

Chapter 9: Time and Certainty

1. Sydney Homer and Richard Sylla, *A History of Interest Rates* (New Brunswick, N.J.: Rutgers University Press, 1996), p. 399; Bank of Canada, Selected Historical Interest Rates at http://www.bank-banque-canada.ca/en/rates/sel_hist.html.

2. See Richard Duncan, *The Dollar Crisis: Causes, Consequences, Cures* (New York: John Wiley & Sons, 2005).

3. See James B. Stewart, *Den of Thieves* (New York: Simon & Schuster, 1991) and Ben Stein, *A License to Steal: The Untold Story of Michael Milken and the Conspiracy to Bilk the Nation* (New York: Simon & Schuster, 1992).

4. "Warren Edward Buffet," *Forbes 400,* October 21, 1991, p. 151.

Chapter 10: Retiring to a Life Away from Canada

1. See Douglas Gray, *Canadian Snowbird Guide* (4th ed.; Toronto: John Wiley & Sons, 2008), p. 262.

2. OECD, Taxation 2002 reported in OECD in Figures: ISBN 9264013059.

Chapter 11: The Future of Retirement

1. Canada, Department of Finance, *Budget 2005,* Annex 3.

2. Sherry Cooper, *The New Retirement* (Toronto: Viking Canada, 2008), p. 75.

Acknowledgments

Numerous people have contributed to *When Can I Retire?*
Financial planners Derek Moran, Caroline Nalbantoglu, Adrian
Mastracci, Dan Stronach, Michael Cherney, Frank Wiginton, and
the partners at Macdonald Shymko & Company are among those
who have contributed to my column, Financial Facelift, at the
Globe and Mail and, by the lessons I have learned in writing that
column, to this book. At the *Globe and Mail*, a succession of
editors, including Dave Pyette, Scott Adams, Marty Cej, Karen
Benzing, and Mike Babad, have worked with me on Financial
Facelift and related columns. Their support has been valuable. For
many insights into retirement plans, I am grateful to Gena Katz,
F.C.A., a tax specialist with Ernst & Young LLP in Toronto. As
well, at *Investment Executive*, my editors Pablo Fuchs, Lara Hertel,
and Tessa Wilmott have supported my work. My friends in the
financial community, including James Cristall, Tanis Bridges, and
Sheila Balasko, have provided assistance. I have been guided by
excellent financial managers, including Tom Czitron of Sceptre
Investment Counsel Ltd.; Jackee Pratt, Craig Allardyce, and Mal
Spooner of Mavrix Fund Management Inc.; Brad Bondy of Genus
Capital Management Inc.; Michael McHugh of Dynamic Funds;
Chris Kresic of Mackenzie Financial Corp.; retiree Mel Rempel;
and my friends Brock Cordes, Bryan Dunlop, Adrian Long, Gary
Thompson, and Casey Van Seters. Their advice has been valuable,
but any errors in *When Can I Retire?* are my own.

I have to express my thanks to my partner, Heather Winters, for her counsel; to my children, Adam and Sarah, for their support; to their partners, Kate Mossman and Dov Secter, for their interest; to my friends Richard Bel and Ida Albo for their patience in hearing out my notions; and to Andrea Magyar, the editorial director at Penguin Group (Canada) for her trust and wisdom. Finally, I have to thank my text editor, Wendy Thomas, for her assistance. As well, I am indebted to my literary agent, Bev Slopen, for support and counsel without which this book would not have been written.

Index